The
END
of
LEADERSHIP

The
END
of
LEADERSHIP

BARBARA KELLERMAN

HARPER
BUSINESS

An Imprint of HarperCollins*Publishers*
www.harpercollins.com

HarperCollins books may be purchased for educational, business, or sales promotional use. For information, please e-mail the Special Markets Department at SPsales@harpercollins.com.

FIRST EDITION

Designed by Michael P. Correy

Library of Congress Cataloging-in-Publication Data has been applied for.

ISBN: 978-0-06-206916-0

17 18 19   OV/RRD   10 9 8 7 6

For Kenneth Dana Greenwald and Thomas Dana Greenwald.

Circling back, full circle, center of the circle.

Change or die.

—CLAUDIAN

Change is inevitable—except from a vending machine.

—ROBERT C. GALLAGHER

Acknowledgments

I owe a debt to Jonathan Greenwald, Kenneth Greenwald, Hollis Heimbouch, Colleen Lawrie, Mike Leveriza, and Todd Pittinsky.

But what exactly I owe them remains to be determined. . . .

Contents

Introduction: Twenty-First-Century Leadership—and Followership

I make my living in "leadership." I have written and edited more than a dozen books on the subject. I have taught leadership at the graduate and undergraduate levels for over thirty years. And I have led or been part of various leadership centers, institutes, and associations. Why then write a book that bites the hand that feeds me? Why take on a profession in which I myself am deeply entrenched? Why pick a fight with many if not most of my colleagues—others who, like me, till this soil, some of whom are good friends and acquaintances?

The reason is that I'm uneasy, increasingly so, about leadership in the twenty-first century and the gap between the teaching of leadership and the practice of leadership. Moreover, I'm downright queasy about what I call the "leadership industry"—my catchall term for the now countless leadership centers, institutes, programs, courses, seminars, workshops, experiences, trainers, books, blogs, articles, websites, webinars, videos, conferences, consultants, and coaches claiming to teach people—usually for money—how to lead.

Being a leader has become a mantra. It is a presumed path to money and power; a medium for achievement, both individual and institutional; and a mechanism for creating change sometimes—though hardly always—for the common good.

But there are other, parallel truths: that leaders of every sort are in disrepute; that the tireless teaching of leadership has brought us no closer to leadership nirvana than we were previously; that we don't have much better an idea of how to grow good leaders, or of how to stop or at least slow bad leaders, than we did a hundred or even a thousand years ago; that the context is changing in ways leaders seem unwilling or unable fully to grasp; that followers are becoming on the one hand disappointed and disillusioned, and on the other entitled, emboldened, and empowered; and, lastly, that notwithstanding the enormous sums of money and time that have been poured into trying to teach people how to lead, over its roughly forty-year history the leadership industry has not in any major, meaningful, measurable way improved the human condition.

I wish I could say that these truths are a matter of only minor importance—of interest only to those of us who make a living from leadership, or to those who pay to learn how to lead. But they are not. I am describing a bigger problem—a gnawing, growing, chronic problem that threatens the fabric of life in the twenty-first century, that undermines whatever the arrangements have been between leaders and followers, and that imposes disorder on a world requiring a modicum of order. Put directly, the leadership industry is much less than meets the eye. For whatever the industry's small, generally narrow successes, humankind writ large is suffering from a crisis of confidence in those who are charged with leading wisely and well, and from a surfeit of mostly well-intentioned but finally false promises made by those supposed to make things better.

None of this is to say that the leadership industry is without merit altogether. Nor is it to say that everyone who purports to teach how to lead is somehow flawed, or that everyone who purports to have learned how to lead is somehow misguided. Rather it is to insist there is a problem—one that is impossible to address without acknowledging it even exists.

Bottom line: while the leadership industry has been thriving—growing and prospering beyond anyone's early imaginings—leaders by and large are performing poorly, worse in many ways than before, miserably disappointing in any case to those among us who once believed the experts held the keys to the kingdom.

Change

Everything is vulnerable to the vicissitudes of change—a general rule to which leadership is no exception. The institution of marriage, of all things, provides an interesting comparison. In mid-eighteenth-century England, a woman's property and children belonged to her husband. Divorce was impossible and, if a wife dared leave home and hearth, she had to leave her children in the process. Moreover, marital rape was perfectly legal and probably frequent—though in 1782 a law finally was passed that forbade a husband to beat his wife with a stick wider than his thumb.[1]

A hundred years later, marriage was different, but only slightly. In 1848, at the Seneca Falls Convention, Elizabeth Cady Stanton charged that marital abuse still remained the norm. She claimed the history of mankind was "a history of repeated injuries . . . on the part of man toward woman. . . . He has made her, if married, in the eye of the law, civilly dead. . . . She is compelled to promise obedience to her husband, he becoming, to all intents and purposes, her master."[2]

By the mid-twentieth century, marriage had changed yet again, particularly in the United States. By then Betty Friedan, author of *The Feminine Mystique*, the so-called bible of the modern women's movement, was able to address a different sort of problem altogether.[3] In fact, her genius was to reveal a truth hiding in plain sight: that though there was nothing obvious for them to be unhappy about, many married women were, nevertheless, deeply unhappy, feeling stifled rather than liberated.

Now, of course, another fifty years on, the institution of marriage has changed yet again. There are further permutations, such as gay marriage, and in its traditional form wives are relatively stronger and husbands relatively weaker. Roughly half of all American marriages end in divorce, and children are more likely to stay with their mothers, not their fathers. Moreover, given that more than 40 percent of children are born to single mothers, and that some 70 percent of mothers now earn their own money, the institution of marriage is considered by many to be more elective than mandatory. In other words, in the last 150 years or so, American marriage has evolved from an arrangement in which wives were subservient to one in which they are nearly, mostly, the equal of their husbands.[4]

Between husbands and wives, and leaders and followers, there is a single striking similarity: patterns of dominance and difference are radically different now from what they were even one hundred years ago, at least in the West. Humankind has always been organized on the assumption that some are weaker while others are stronger. Between men and women, it was presumed until only recently that husbands would, and should, dominate, while wives would, and should, defer. But as historian Stephanie Coontz points out, marriage now is different. It is expected to be free of the coercion, violence, and gender inequities that in the past were commonplace.[5] Along similar lines, between leaders and followers it was presumed until only recently that leaders should dominate and followers defer. Leaders were generally expected to tell followers what to do, and followers were generally expected to do as they were told. No longer. Now followers, like wives, are far sturdier than they used to be, stronger and more independent. Moreover, now, ideally anyway, leaders are supposed to suggest or recommend that their followers follow, not order them to do so.

Let's go back to the late eighteenth century, to that time of upheaval when the ideas of the Enlightenment were beginning to be realized. Patterns of dominance and deference were changing in marriage and, simultaneously, they were changing in the body politic. The two most obvious examples are the American Revolution and the French Revolution. Both were transformational events in which followers came to the fore, while leaders came under attack. In Europe and America, life—political, economic, and social—was never again the same.

Nor was it coincidence that some fifty years later, as Stanton was penning *her* list of grievances by the powerless (women) against the powerful (men), Karl Marx and Friedrich Engels were penning *their* list of grievances by the powerless (the proletariat) against the powerful (bourgeoisie). Indeed just as the year was precisely the same—both Stanton's "Declaration of Sentiments" and Marx and Engels's *Communist Manifesto* were published in 1848—the point was precisely the same. A half century after the American and French revolutions large numbers of followers remained restive—eager to change their status as subordinates.

Not until 1920 did American women receive the right to vote. And not until 1917 was there a Russian (a successful) communist revolution. Nevertheless, the arc of modern history begins to become clear. Since the time of the Enlightenment, *because* of the Enlightenment, the weak increasingly challenged the strong. Less than fifty years after the Russian Revolution, 1963 to be precise, Martin Luther King Jr. wrote his seminal "Letter from Birmingham Jail," and, of course, Friedan published her seminal *Feminine*

Mystique. As King intended to upend relations between whites and blacks by empowering blacks, Friedan intended to upend relations between men and women by empowering wives. But the push for equity and empowerment did not end there: in the United States a whole host of other activists eventually signed on and joined in, with the powerless continuing to challenge the powerful right through the late 1960s and early '70s. In campus protests across the country, students took on the academic establishment for various reasons, including free speech and freedom to choose their curricula; and in street protests clear across the country, anti–Vietnam War activists took on the political establishment. In short order other rights revolutions followed—gay rights, disability rights, animal rights, you name it—the whole dynamic changing in less than a decade the balance of power between leaders and followers.

But this expansion of democratization was by no means limited to the United States and Europe. Similar demands were being made elsewhere, such as in Africa, where struggles for independence permeated the continent. For centuries colonizers, mainly Europeans, had controlled the colonized, mainly Africans. Now, by the late 1950s and early '60s, Ghanaians and Kenyans, for example, had had enough. Taking advantage of Europe's debilitation after World War II, large numbers of Africans used whatever means necessary to throw off the yoke of their oppression.

Since then leadership and followership have continued to evolve—including during the last thirty to forty years, which are the focus of this book—from what they were into something quite different. More nations now are democracies as opposed to autocracies. There is less respect for authority across the board—in government and business, in the academy and in the professions, even in religion. Power and influence have continued to devolve from the top down—those at the top having less power and influence; those in the middle and at the bottom having more. For their part, followers, ordinary people, have an expanded sense of entitlement—demanding more and giving less. There has been a revolution in the use of technology as a tool and, partly in consequence, the playing field has been leveled, in both groups and organizations. Finally there has been explosive growth—in the leadership industry.

Here and Now

The leadership industry—which remains largely though no longer entirely an American phenomenon—is a focus of this book. There is no point in mincing words: whatever the difference it has made at the micro level—which in some cases is no doubt real, for example, within individuals and within individual groups and organizations—at the macro level its deficits loom large. Instead of making our leaders more effective and ethical, it seems at least to have had the opposite effect—it seems to have made things worse. American government and business are suffering from a near breakdown in their capacity creatively and collaboratively to effect policies to address the most pressing of the nation's problems.[6] Levels of trust in and approval of leaders are at all-time lows. And observers such as *New York Times* columnist David Brooks reflect the mood of the moment when they denounce as "fundamentally self-dealing" not one leader in particular, but the entire "leadership class."[7]

Obviously there is no one-to-one correlation. It's not as if every corporate executive and every top government official has taken a leadership course. Moreover, most of those who engage in leader learning do testify, albeit subjectively, to the efficacy of their experience. Still, if Americans are so good at developing leaders, why is America in such a mess? Why are our politics so ineffectual and why is our economy so resistant to resilience? Can those of us in the leadership industry honestly say that, in the last several decades, we have had the impact we wanted and intended?

Part of the problem is with mistaken assumptions. We think leadership is static—it is not. We think leadership can be taught—which, given the paucity of objective evidence, might be true or might not. We think leadership can be learned quickly and easily and that one form of leadership can be taught, simultaneously, to different people in different situations—a stretch at best. We think of context as being of secondary or even tertiary importance—which is wrongheaded. We think leader-centrically—that being a leader is better and more important than being a follower. Wrong again.

This book, then, tells two tales. The first is about leadership and change. It is about how and why leadership and followership have evolved over time. And about how and why leadership and followership have continued to evolve, especially in the last forty years. My emphasis is on the American experience, but my canvas is large, encompassing leadership and followership worldwide.

The second is about the leadership industry itself. It explores what the industry is exactly, and what its mainstream ideologies and pedagogies are. It explains how leader learning is supposedly accomplished and asks, finally, what we can reasonably conclude about its various efforts. How, in other words, should we assess the leadership industry and what, more particularly, has it accomplished, or failed to?

But to begin, some markers to position my prose:

First I define *follower*—a word I use frequently—simply by rank. That is, followers are subordinates who have less power, authority, and influence than do their superiors, and who therefore usually, but not invariably, fall into line.[8] They are divided into five different types, according to their level of engagement: *Isolates* do not care about their leaders, or know anything about them, or respond to them in any way. *Bystanders* do care, but they make a deliberate decision to stand aside, to disengage from their leaders and from whatever is the group dynamic. *Participants* are in some way involved, clearly favoring their leaders or clearly opposed. *Activists* feel strongly about their leaders, one way or another, and they act accordingly, investing heavily in people and process. And *Diehards* are, as their name implies, prepared to die for their leaders—or, conversely, to oust them by any means necessary.[9]

Second, I consider *context* equally as important as leaders and followers. Think of my model as an equilateral triangle—with leaders, followers, and context each along one, similar, side. In keeping with this model, all three are, in effect, equally weighted on every page of this book.

Third, I distinguish among power, authority, and influence. *Power* is defined here as A's capacity to get B to do whatever A wants, whatever B's preference, and if necessary by force. *Authority* is A's capacity to get B to do whatever A wants, based on A's position, status, or rank. And *influence* is as it sounds: A's capacity to persuade B to go along with what A wants and intends, of B's own volition.

Fourth, again, I focus extensively but by no means exclusively on the United States. I intend for the argument to be overarching—to address patterns of dominance and deference worldwide.[10] So, though the United States is at the center of the action, the assumption is globalization, that what happens in one place affects and is affected by what happens in another.

Fifth, I avoid like the plague definitions of leadership (of which, at last count, there were some fifteen hundred) and theories of leadership (of which there are around forty).[11] Instead I keep it simple: I assume that leadership development implies developing good leaders, and that good leaders are both ethical and effective.

Finally, a note about the title of this book: it is meant as a caution about the future of leadership in the twenty-first century. For nearly everywhere, leaders are found wanting, followers are restive, and the context is changing—sometimes at warp speed. So unless we get a grip, the prognosis is grim.

But while "getting a grip" is difficult, it is not impossible. As we will see, there are ways to enhance and elevate the leadership industry—to make it completely contemporaneous by being broadly based rather than narrowly focused, by being inclusive rather than exclusive. Moreover, there are ways to educate women and men so they learn to be good, smart followers as well as good, smart leaders, and develop as large a capacity for contextual intelligence as for emotional intelligence. Leading is, as we know by now, different from what it was before, even a decade or two ago. And as it changes, so must the leadership industry, lest it be relegated to the dustbin of history.

Part I

Power Shift

1

Historical Trajectory—
lessening power

L eadership has a long history and a clear trajectory. More than anything else it is about the devolution of power—from those up top to those down below.

On High

In the beginning we had gods and goddesses. They were heroes, or hero-leaders, removed from ordinary people and quotidian concerns, to be venerated and emulated and fixated on—notwithstanding an Achilles' heel or even fatal flaw. Some hero-leaders were imagined, for example, the Greek god Zeus, and his daughter Athena. Others were (or thought to be) real, men such as Abraham, Buddha, Jesus, and Mohammed.

Hero-leaders are part of our collective psyche—they serve a psychological purpose. Mythologist Joseph Campbell wrote, "Freud, Jung, and their followers have demonstrated irrefutably that the logic, the heroes, and the deeds of myth survive into modern times."[1] Freud certainly was fixated on both leadership and followership, convinced not only that "the leader of the group is still the dreaded primal father," but that the group itself, all groups, long for a strong leader. "The group," he maintained, "has an extreme passion for authority"; and individuals have "a thirst for obedience."[2] Similarly, Jung developed a heroic archetype, a hero-leader who appears and reappears, everywhere, throughout human history.

The heroes of myth and legend, otherworldly and oddly familiar at the same time, become so only after battling demons and emerging triumphant, if scathed and inexorably changed. Campbell writes, "A hero ventures forth from the world of common day into a region of supernatural wonder: fabulous forces are there encountered and a decisive victory is won: the hero comes back from this mysterious adventure with the power to bestow boons on his fellow man."[3]

Lest this voyage to elsewhere and back seem impossibly remote, separate and distinct from our own mundane lives, think of recent hero-leaders such as Martin Luther King Jr. and Nelson Mandela, both of whom survived stretches in solitary confinement and, in Mandela's case, long incarceration, only to emerge from their ordeals more powerful as leaders than ever. Or think even of Apple's iconic CEO, the late Steve Jobs, who, after first being fired and later fighting pancreatic cancer, which is nearly always lethal, returned, repeatedly, until he could no longer do so, to lead his company and produce products more wondrous than their predecessors.

Our longing for a hero-leader is, then, ancient and simultaneously completely contemporaneous.[4] When nineteenth-century philosopher Thomas Carlyle wrote of great men, great leaders, he invoked the word *hero* and exalted the "heroic" in history. "We have undertaken to discourse here . . . on what I call Hero-worship and the Heroic in human affairs."[5] And when countless numbers of Americans screamed and stomped for Barack Obama during the 2008 presidential campaign, it reflected widespread wishful thinking—that here was a hero for our own times, a Great Man who had overcome great odds (most obviously his being an African American) to create change and cure what ails us. In a typical scene a month before the election, in Columbus, Missouri, lines formed early for a nighttime rally. Thousands gathered to pack tightly around the stage on which Obama would appear, and thousands more circled a huge, larger-than-life screen that promised his likeness. Video cameras were held high to capture the moment, while throngs shifted, hoping to catch a glimpse of the man himself, of the human incarnation of "the audacity of hope."[6]

Of course the hero-leader has a counterpart—the monster-leader. Our vulnerability to leaders who turn out to be tyrants is as old as the proverbial hills—and remains a human conundrum. Sometimes the tyrant is clearly distinguishable and immediately recognizable as a menace. Campbell writes that the "figure of the tyrant-monster is known to the mythologies, folk traditions, legends, and even nightmares, of the world; and his characteristics are everywhere essentially the same. He is the hoarder of the general benefit. He is the monster avid for the greedy rights of 'my and mine.' "[7] But there are other times when the monster-leader is less obvious, hidden even, because he and the hero-leader are one and the same. During the 1930s, Hitler was on the one hand revered as a hero-leader by millions of Germans who were in total thrall to the power of his persona. As one early Nazi sympathizer put it after hearing Hitler speak, "My critical faculty was swept away . . . I experienced an exaltation that could only be likened to a religious conversion. . . . I had found myself, my leader, and my cause."[8] On the other hand there were others who recognized early on that Hitler was a monster-leader—the difference in the eye of the beholder.

Freud himself (who was forced by the Nazis to go into exile in England) was stunned that in twentieth-century Germany a leader like Hitler could exert such power, could have such a hold on his people. "How," Freud asked in his last book, which at the obvious level was about Moses, "is it possible that one single man can develop such extraordinary effectiveness, can develop out of indifferent individuals and families *one* people?" To his own question he provided an answer: "We know that the great majority of people have a strong need for authority which they can admire . . . and which dominates and sometimes even ill-treats them."⁹

But, notwithstanding our apparently innate inclination to hero worship, over the centuries our attitudes toward governance evolved. Generally they became somewhat more grounded and pragmatic, more preoccupied with this world and less with other worlds, whatever they might be. Moreover to the problem of who should lead to maintain order and keep the peace, Confucius and Plato, who were approximate contemporaries (400–500 BCE), had the essentially same solution: find extraordinary men and provide them an extraordinary education so they learn to lead wisely and well.

Confucius believed in cultivating leaders who were "gentlemen," who possessed *de*, which is to say, virtue. Confucius's ideal leader was, in modern parlance, a role model, a gentleman to be emulated, and finally followed, because he was older, wiser, better. His capacity to lead was based on moral suasion: he attracted followers by setting an example, by himself being as close to perfect as possible; and then presiding over rites and rituals that were symbols of stability and security.

Confucius was asked, "How does one qualify to govern?" The Master answered, "He who cultivates the five treasures and eschews the four evils is fit to govern." Next he was questioned, "What are the five treasures?" To this Confucius replied, "A gentleman is generous without having to spend; he makes people work without having them groan; he has ambition but no rapacity; he has authority but no arrogance; he is stern but not fierce."¹⁰

Plato's ideal leader, the philosopher-king, seems on the surface to have little in common with Confucius's ideal leader, the gentleman. Whereas a gentleman is virtuous above all, the philosopher-king is virtuous—and then some. The product of an intense and extended, even lifelong education, the philosopher-king is exceptional in every aspect, a ruler who is a philosopher, a philosopher who is a ruler, a perfect leader trained over a lifetime to lead cautiously and cleverly, seriously and sensibly, in a realm of truth and beauty.

Not incidentally, Plato's philosopher-king has a fully realized counterpart, a monster-leader whom Plato terms a tyrant. Of him he writes, "He is the joint product of his tyrannical nature and his despotic rule, and the longer he rules, the more oppressive his tyranny." Given the times in which he lived, small wonder that Plato's philosopher-king is an ideal to be conjured, whereas his tyrant is real, a man to be feared. And, given the times in which he lived, small wonder that Plato believed that unless "philosophers become kings in our cities, or unless those who now are kings and rulers become true philosophers . . . there can be no end to our troubles."[11]

Still, differences notwithstanding, Confucius's gentleman leader and Plato's philosopher-king have key characteristics in common: they approximate perfection; they crown a context that is leader-centric; and they are of an historical moment in which good governance seemed completely to depend on good, even great leadership. In the history of leadership, therefore, they belong to a time when it was widely believed that only hero-leaders, great men of singular virtue and accomplishment, could save us from ourselves.

Down to Earth

After eons in which leader-power was or seemed near-total, there was, finally, a limit on leadership. In 1215, King John of England was obliged to sign the Magna Carta, obliged formally to accept that his authority was not absolute and his will could not be arbitrarily exercised. It was a turning point in the history of leadership—and a turning point in the history of followership. The king was forced to sign the document by some of his subjects, noblemen determined to protect their personal and political privileges, first through a council and later though an increasingly powerful parliament. The signing of the Magna Carta was a watershed in Western history, in which the leader was compelled to succumb to his followers, who came together and stayed together until they had gotten their way with His Majesty.

Change was slow. This was, after all, still the Middle Ages, when royalty ruled here on earth and when God, through the authority of the Catholic Church, ruled the kingdom of heaven (at least in the West). It was all the more remarkable, then, that during the early Renaissance there emerged arguably the greatest leadership theorist of all—one whose secularism and pragmatism pertain to this day.

Niccolò Machiavelli's *The Prince* (1513) has justly been called the most famous book on politics ever written. Machiavelli's hardnosed, astute advice to his leader, his prince, is so much a product of his preternatural understanding of the human condition, and so free of frippery, it will forever be universal in its application, one of the few great works of literature to transcend time and place.

The Prince has a special place in the history of leadership as well: it was the first significant treatise on leadership to concern itself exclusively with what was real, rather than ideal. Machiavelli did not, as did Confucius and Plato, dwell in the realm of the perfect. In fact, as God is absent from *The Prince*, so is the rule of law and so for that matter is a moral compass of any kind. Machiavelli's prince is embedded in the here and now. He is self-aware and self-contained, impervious to outside influence, including from on high. He is single-minded and single-tracked, interested above all in securing first the preservation of his power, then the preservation of his principality, and finally the preservation of peace among his people. (Machiavelli's opinion of the human condition was low. He described the prince's subjects as being "ungrateful, fickle, pretenders and dissemblers, evaders of danger, eager for gain.")[12]

But however brilliant was *The Prince*, it was not Machiavelli who finally broke with the past. Rather it was Thomas Hobbes. It was Hobbes who proposed an arrangement between leaders and followers that was new and different altogether.

Like their predecessors Confucius and Plato, Machiavelli and Hobbes shared a single overriding concern: how to maintain order in a disorderly world. But Machiavelli was part of an earlier tradition, in which the fixation was on the person in power. Hobbes was more expansive: he turned his attention from those with power to those without, particularly regarding their right, our right, to life. It was a sea change. For the first time in the history of Western thought, at least one claim of the ruled superseded in importance the claim of the ruler. As philosopher Leo Strauss observed, the change from an orientation by natural duties to an orientation by natural rights finds its most potent expression in the ideas of Hobbes, who put the unconditional right to life at the center of his argument.[13]

Like Machiavelli, Hobbes believed that man was not to be trusted—he was fearful and rapacious, selfish and dangerous. Moreover, like Machiavelli, whom he succeeded by not much more than a hundred years, Hobbes believed that the best leader was authoritarian, someone with power and authority sufficient to control those otherwise unable or unwilling to control themselves. But, *un*like Machiavelli, Hobbes had an embryonic conception of what later came to be called a social contract. The arrangement that Hobbes proposed was this: Followers would grant absolute power to an absolute leader who would give them something in exchange. Through the state, he would provide them with protection—first to secure the right to life, and second to provide for a life well lived, one that, as Hobbes put it, was "commodious" and occasionally even "delightful."

Like all histories, the history of leadership is one of intrusions and interruptions. So the phenomenon of which I write—the power shift from top to bottom—did not follow a linear path. Some three hundred years had to pass between the signing of the Magna Carta in 1215 and Martin Luther's historic challenge to the absolute authority of the Catholic Church. (For centuries the church controlled access even to the Bible, available in the Middle Ages only in Latin. Thus only scholar-priests who read Latin had the right to read it; ordinary people, who did not read Latin, did not.) Moreover, the first modern revolution—the so-called Glorious Revolution in England, which demolished the idea that kings rule by "divine right"—did not take place until 1688.

Just as Hobbes's ideas on relations between ruler and ruled signaled a break with the past, so did the Glorious Revolution. A few salient points: First, real revolutions are rare and distinctive events, which fundamentally alter the state or society within which they take place. Second, the intention of revolutionaries is generally to redistribute power, authority, and influence, by taking some, or even all, from those who have and giving it to those who do not. Third, as Steve Pincus has pointed out, "the Revolution of 1688–89 was the first modern revolution not only because it transformed English state and society but also because, like all modern revolutions, it was *popular, violent, and divisive.* The revolutionaries of 1688–89 numbered in the thousands. They were not a tiny political elite."[14] Fourth, this particular revolution was a necessary precursor to the great late-eighteenth-century revolutions that would take place in America and France.

The Glorious Revolution was, then, a turning point in the history of leadership and followership, and a foreshadowing of greater change yet to come. The fact that this particular upheaval was the first that can reasonably be described as "popular," the first in which relatively large numbers of followers were bound and determined to diminish their leaders, makes it a historical event important in its own right, as well as a harbinger of a future for followers that was far different from their past.

All Hell Breaks Loose

While democracy in ancient Athens has long been fabled, the Greek experiment in participatory government was actually short-lived. It took another two thousand years for the rights of the led to be irrevocably, enduringly encoded in political theory and practice. Until the seventeenth and eighteenth centuries, it was the leader who was at the center of the action, just as, until Copernicus in the sixteenth century, it was the earth around which revolved everything else.

John Locke was born in 1632, less than fifty years after Thomas Hobbes. But his work on the relationship between leaders and led was a great leap forward. As I've written elsewhere, "Locke's logic concerning the right to hold private property; his conception of social contract theory, which claims that governments derive their legitimacy from the consent of the governed; and his insistence that this consent be applied to the leader as well as to the led—all were breakthroughs. In fact, Locke's [declaration] that if the leader does not sufficiently satisfy the led, he may be recalled, by force if necessary, puts him finally completely at odds with Hobbes, who, except in matters of life and death, would have had us surrender to an absolute authority with absolute power."15

More than any other single thinker, with the possible exception of Montesquieu, Locke provided the moral, legal, and philosophical basis for a system of governance based on a reasonably equitable distribution of power between leaders and led. Of particular interest here is the continuing evolution of the idea of a social contract. Locke argued that such a contract should be expansive, going much further than did Hobbes in bestowing on followers power at the expense of leaders. The power and authority of leaders were to be limited. And people not in positions of power and authority were to be given the right, under certain circumstances, to unseat those who were, if necessary by force.

Additionally, though Locke was not alone in developing the doctrine of the separation of powers, he made such a strong case for balancing the power of government by placing several parts of it in different hands that he solidified the idea of distributed leadership, as opposed to centralized leadership. Finally Locke was a pioneer on the subject of property, on the right of ordinary people to reap what they sowed. This alone was an important step in the evolution of political and economic thought, and a further impingement by the have-nots on the rights of the haves.

Nowhere was Locke more appreciated, or more influential, than on the North American continent. During the prerevolutionary period his books were widely circulated, and when the Declaration of Independence was signed, it was judged so derivative that Jefferson was actually accused of copying Locke's *Second Treatise of Government*.

By the time the Enlightenment was in full flower, Locke was dead. But he foreshadowed what throughout the Western world became a time of great change—in arts and sciences, in culture and government, and in political thought, especially as it pertained to patterns of dominance and deference. For if the Age of Enlightenment was about anything, it was about casting doubt on what previously had been presumed our proper place here on earth and in the kingdom of heaven. Old values were challenged. New ones—especially with regard to who had the right to do what to whom—took their place. Historian Peter Gay argued that the Enlightenment broke through what he called "the sacred circle," the interdependent relationship between European aristocracy and the hierarchy of the Catholic Church. It was precisely the intrusion on the sacred circle, and, ultimately its dissolution, that heralded the end of one era in relations between leaders and followers and the beginning of another.

Portents were everywhere, especially in England and France, and in North America. Then came two explosions: the American Revolution, whose apotheosis was the Declaration of Independence, drafted in 1776; and the French Revolution, whose apotheosis was the first French Republic, declared in 1792. Both revolutions upended rulers in favor of the ruled. Both compelled the aristocracy to establish a semblance of a democracy. And both distributed power, authority, and influence much more widely than they had been distributed before.

Unlike their European counterparts, who had a history of hierarchy, Americans had never had a monarch, an absolute authority of any kind, except at great remove. Still, the level of anti-authority sentiment among the colonists was high as they responded with growing anger at British officials who they believed treated them like second-class subjects. Thomas Paine, author of *Common Sense*, which sparked the flame that lit the revolution, reflected this rage at the crown. He accused "the King and his parasites" of every evil, reminding Americans that by leaving Great Britain their ancestors had fled "not from the tender embraces of the mother, but from the cruelty of the monster." Nor, Paine claimed, was England done with dirty deeds: "The same tyranny which drove the first emigrants from home, pursues their descendents still."[16]

Paine's readers were receptive. The American Revolution was not only about hero-leaders, about founders such as Washington, Adams, Jefferson, and Madison. It was a genuinely popular uprising, in which large numbers of people ultimately participated. T. H. Breen writes: "The evidence of ordinary Americans mobilizing in response to parliamentary insults and an army of occupation, forging common bonds of sympathy throughout all thirteen colonies, and creating an infrastructure to support and drive forward revolution in the years ahead of the Declaration of Independence is overwhelming."[17]

The insurgents were plain people, mostly from white farm families who made up some 70 percent of the free inhabitants of colonial America. They were, in other words, followers—Participants, Activists, and in some cases Diehards—ordinary people ready, willing, and able to invest some or even all of what they had to oust the power on the throne.[18]

America's revolutionary genesis had effects that were permanent and pervasive—it shaped American ideas on followership as well as leadership. In revolutionary times resistance is a virtue and obedience a vice, which is why, as historian Bernard Bailyn described it, defiance during the revolutionary period "poured from the colonial presses and was hurled from half the pulpits of the land. The right, the need, the absolute obligation to disobey legally constituted authority had become the universal cry."[19] A consequence of this antagonism was anti-authoritarianism—an attitude that persists to this day. Even now Americans tend to be suspicious of government, ambivalent toward those in positions of power.

This prejudice against power and authority is embedded in what political scientist Samuel Huntington called the American Creed. What is the implication of ideas, ideals such as equality, liberty, individualism, constitutionalism, and democracy? They all impose limits on power. "Opposition to power," wrote Huntington, "and suspicion of government as the most dangerous embodiment of power, are the central themes of American political thought."[20]

Of course opposition to power was by no means limited to the American experience. During the nineteenth century, throughout Europe as well as the United States, the earlier establishment was everywhere upended or, at the least, threatened. Most important, the fortunes of two groups that heretofore were generally enslaved and oppressed, blacks and women, changed dramatically. Slavery and also serfdom were finally abolished everywhere in Europe and America, and women slowly but certainly demanded basic rights, such as the right to vote. Moreover, nearly everywhere in the West, the now rapidly expanding working class formed the rudiments of a trade union movement. While this movement did not ultimately mature into an international alliance, over time working people did develop some sense of self-worth and self-interest.

As groups staked their claim, so in time did individuals. In 1849, Henry David Thoreau published a piece, "Resistance to Civil Government," that was all about the rights and responsibilities of individuals. It was all about my right, and yours, to be heard, and about my responsibility, and yours, to do no wrong, no matter the instruction from someone more highly positioned. "I think that we should be individuals first, and subjects second," wrote Thoreau. "The only obligation which I have a right to assume is to do at any time what I think right."[21]

But it was John Stuart Mill's essay *On Liberty* that most famously celebrated the rights of individuals—everyone's right to do as they pleased so long as they did not intrude on the rights of anyone else. Mill, like Thoreau a decade before, downplayed the importance of, even the need for, leadership. Mill traced the trajectory of power, noting there had come a time "in the progress of human affairs, when men ceased to think it a necessity of nature that their governors should be an independent power, opposed in interest to themselves." Mill argued that though this was progress, the time was now to take another step forward. The time was now for near-total autonomy, near-total freedom: "Neither one person, nor any number of persons, is warranted in saying to another human creature of ripe years, that he shall not do with his own life for his own benefit what he chooses to do with it."[22]

Leadership and followership had come a long way—in just a hundred fifty years. Through evolution and revolution, the balance between those who had power, authority, and influence and those who did not had changed in ways that would never, could never, be undone.

Bottom's Up

In the last one hundred years, relations between leaders and followers reached a turning point, if not a tipping point. Leader power and follower power became the more equivalent. To be sure, hero-leaders (Franklin Roosevelt, Winston Churchill) and monster-leaders (Adolf Hitler, Joseph Stalin) were still in evidence. But, increasingly, ordinary people joined forces to compel change the world over.

Early in his life Mohandas Gandhi was a lawyer. Later in his life it became his mission, his passion, to liberate India from British colonial rule. Idiosyncratic and peripatetic, Gandhi's crusade began in South Africa, where as a young man he had had an experience that, it was said, changed him forever. Shortly after his arrival from India in 1893 he was thrown off a train on account of his color. His humiliation prompted his growing political involvement, his growing interest in how the powerless might wrest respect and everything it implied from the powerful. The result was *satyagraha*—"truth-force" or "soul-force," a political principle and practice available to anyone, no matter their station.

Satyagraha involves the use of nonviolent resistance in order to resolve conflict through conciliation, as opposed to conquest. "Satyagraha," Gandhi wrote, "is not physical force. A *satyagrahi* does not inflict pain on the adversary; he does not seek his destruction. A *satyagrahi* never resorts to firearms. In the use of *satyagraha*, there is no ill will whatsoever."[43] Disclaimers notwithstanding, nor protestations of truth and love, there was no mistaking the intent of *satyagraha*. It was a political weapon or, if you prefer, a political tool or tactic, one of the few available to have-nots to use against haves.

When Gandhi returned to India in 1915, he did what he had done in South Africa. He used *satyagraha* to bring about change, to bring about an end to India's colonial subjugation. The turning point was in 1930, when Gandhi led the legendary salt *satyagraha*, a mass protest against the British for imposing a tax on salt. By the time it was over, the British raj had changed forever. Though colonial rule in India formally came to an end only in 1947, Gandhi's decision seventeen years earlier to launch a nationwide nonviolent protest, to tap into the power of the people and marshal it against the power of the British Empire, was decisive. It made evident that though they were relatively powerless, Indians in growing numbers were willing to risk arrest and worse in the fight for independence.

Nelson Mandela started out a disciple of Gandhi. Early on, during the 1940s and early '50s, he believed that nonviolent resistance might work in South Africa, might change relations between the white minority that was dominant and the black majority that was, of necessity, deferent. But after he was arrested in 1956 for political opposition, and then again in 1962, Mandela changed. In the mid-1960s he was rearrested and, after a two-year trial, he was sentenced to life imprisonment for acts of violence against the government of South Africa.

During his final trial Mandela was given a chance to speak in court, which he did, at length, delivering in 1964 what turned out to be the most eloquent of all his political speeches. He spoke of how even when the odds against them were long, the weak still could, and should, take on the strong. He spoke of how he and his colleagues had tried nonviolence—to no avail. Finally he spoke of how he had no choice but to turn to violence to force a measure of equity between those with power and authority and those without.

Mandela was freed from prison in 1990, and in 1994, as the result of South Africa's first multiracial democratic election, he became president. South African oppression had come to an end as a result of pressures both internal and external, signaling finally the close of an era. For throughout the second half of the twentieth century, liberation movements such as those in India and South Africa became nearly commonplace, especially in Asia and Africa. Majorities from Algeria to Laos, from Ghana to Rhodesia were simply no longer willing to do what they had done for so long—defer to minorities who were outsiders.

Nor did the thrust for independence diminish as the century came to a close. The Soviet Union collapsed, leading to a slew of new, independent states, Georgia, Belarus, and Kazakhstan, for example, that for decades had been Soviet socialist republics. Moreover, other European countries, ones that nominally were independent but nevertheless under Soviet hegemony, from Latvia to Romania, broke free of Russia's iron grip. A series of so-called bloodless revolutions—from the Velvet Revolution in Czechoslovakia (1989) to the Orange Revolution in Ukraine (2004)—all were a product of the same phenomenon. Zbigniew Brzezinski described it as a "global political awakening," which was "socially massive, politically radicalizing, and geographically universal."[24]

Change in the United States took a different form, but still it was powerful and consequential. As mentioned, the civil rights movement was only one of several mid- to late-twentieth-century rights movements, each one of which was from the bottom up. Though they were not generally revolutionary in their intent, the demand for change was everywhere in the air and it was not to be easily dismissed. The result: a permanent change in American manners and morals.

Like Mandela, King was a disciple of Gandhi. Thus the inevitable tension: on the one hand King and the movement he inspired were intent on avoiding the incendiary; on the other hand they were impatient to the point of no return. King's "Letter from Birmingham Jail" epitomizes this exquisite balance. First there was this: "In any nonviolent campaign there are four basic steps: collection of the facts . . . ; negotiation; self-purification; and direct action." Then there was this: "We know through painful experience that freedom is never voluntarily given by the oppressor; it must be demanded by the oppressed. . . . There comes a time when the cup of endurance runs over, and men are no longer willing to be plunged into the abyss of despair."[25]

By 1963, King's letter and Friedan's *Feminine Mystique* had been published. Following these came the "Free Speech" movement at the University of California in Berkeley; widespread protests against the Vietnam War; passage of the Architectural Barriers Act, which required all buildings constructed, altered, or financed by the federal government to be accessible to people with disabilities; the first significant gay rights protest (at the Stonewall Inn, in New York City); and the publication of *Animal Liberation*, Peter Singer's "bible" of the animal rights movement.

The 1960s and '70s changed relations between leaders and followers forever, first in the United States and then elsewhere. Individuals and groups without power, authority, or influence— individuals and groups heretofore at the margins—experienced a new sense of entitlement from which nearly no one was exempt: not women or African Americans or the sick or mentally or physically impaired, not gays or lesbians or, later, transgendered, not the young or the old, not even animals.

Radical politics, grassroots politics, citizen politics, participatory politics, grassroots protests, street protests, grassroots activists, citizen activists, community organizers, community action, radical action, affirmative action, political action, democracy in action—the old rules were out the window. Leaders were threatened and followers emboldened, and philosophers like Brazilian Paulo Freire were heard loud and clear: "Who are better prepared than the oppressed to understand the terrible significance of an oppressive society? Who suffer the effects of oppression more than the oppressed? Who can better understand the necessity of liberation?"[26]

Game's Changed

Followers on the rise, leaders in decline—while the trend could be traced back over hundreds of years, in the 1960s and '70s it accelerated, again particularly in the United States. Among other reasons, our most prominent leaders, especially but not exclusively our presidents, were under siege. President John F. Kennedy was assassinated in 1963. Five years later Robert F. Kennedy and Martin Luther King Jr. were shot dead. It continued: the animus against President Lyndon Johnson (on account of the war in Vietnam) obliged him to withdraw from presidential politics. Richard Nixon was forced to resign as president because of the Watergate scandal. And despite their various virtues, both Presidents Gerald Ford and Jimmy Carter lost their respective presidential elections, Ford for his first full term and Carter for his second.

The polls confirmed the malaise. Between 1958 and 1964 the figures on trust in government were high and hardly changed. But during the subsequent decade, antigovernment sentiment grew dramatically. By 1974, the number of Americans who thought (most) politicians were crooked had climbed to 45 percent. Moreover, this loss of faith in political leaders was mirrored by a loss of faith in corporate leaders. During the 1950s and '60s American business was riding high. The corporate sector was self-confident in the extreme: corporate leaders, in turn, were widely perceived as a cut above, tough, rugged, and fully in command. In 1956, *Fortune* magazine described Roger Blough, the chairman of U.S. Steel, as "modest" and "careful," with a "capacious mind, abundantly stocked with differentiated facts. . . . Probably no man has more intimate knowledge of [U.S. Steel's] strengths and weaknesses, or a clearer idea of what might be done about them." Similarly (also in 1956), Harlow Curtice, chairman of General Motors, was described as the perfect "prophet of American expansionism." He was "a trim, tailored man who moves and gestures with athletic grace. He has quite the appropriate degree of vibrancy for a man of affairs . . . and jaw line [that] suggests the aggressive perfectionist that he certainly is."[27]

But by the 1970s, just as damage had been done to America's political leaders, there were chinks in the armor of America's corporate leaders. For instance the automobile industry, which long was at the apex of American business, seemed suddenly, star-tlingly vulnerable to other companies in other countries, especially Germany and Japan. America's economic supremacy was being challenged; in time, so would its political supremacy. Fuel emis-sion regulations, oil shortages, and lack of innovations—all spelled trouble for American cars, which never again so completely domi-nated the global car market.

But the automobile industry was only one example of a problem more widespread. As a 1982 article in *Fortune* detailed, "hard times" had caught up with executives all across corporate America. In the 1970s top managers were still accustomed to "hearty pay increases and an every richer banquet of benefits." Now companies were freezing and cutting salaries, postponing and reducing raises, and suspending bonuses and cost-of-living increases. Moreover, corpo-rate leaders themselves were being scrutinized. Robert Townsend's 1970 blockbuster book, *Up the Organization: How to Stop the Corpora-tion from Stifling People and Strangling Profits*, began what turned out to be a continuing conversation: about how traditional corporate hierarchies were dated, about how large organizations were often cumbersome and inefficient, and about how CEOs were stuck, clinging to old ways of leading and managing when it was obvious they no longer worked.

Even followers—particularly white-collar workers—were being conceived of in ways new and different. A 1971 article in the *Harvard Business Review* titled "Who Wants Corporate Democracy?" pointed out that phrases such as "bottom-up control," "employee activism," and "corporate democracy" were being heard with increasing fre-quency: "All the signs point to an ever-more persistent drive on the part of employees to participate further in the making of corporate policy. . . . Pressures are building to change the rules of corporate governance."[28]

So one could reasonably argue that just as the United States was in some ways in the vanguard in the last decades of the eighteenth century, it was in some ways in the vanguard in the last decades of the twentieth. Some two hundred years after the American Revolution, there was similar ferment—the powerless taking on the powerful, demanding, finally, greater equity.

What, then, can we conclude about the historical trajectory? We can say what we have seen: that over the course of human history, power and influence generally have devolved from the top down. Still, for whatever reasons, the leadership industry ignores this critical history nearly entirely, as if it were irrelevant, or unimportant, or maybe both. One of the several inevitable results is that leaders continue to be overvalued and followers undervalued. The same can be said of the contemporary context—which remains similarly underappreciated and poorly understood. This deprivation serves no one, least of all those learning how to lead.

2

Cultural Constraints—
leveling the playing field

Until recently, someone like me—a professor in an institution of higher education—would have been addressed as "Professor" or "Doctor." Now I'm sometimes called "Professor Kellerman"—and sometimes "Barbara." Similarly, we used to defer to physicians; we'd take their word as gospel and do what they told us to do. Now we pocket their instructions and then second-guess them by getting another opinion, or by getting another ten thousand opinions on WebMD. More generally, once upon a time we simply obeyed orders issued by our superiors, our leaders and managers. Now we incline more to challenge them, emboldened to do so by the spread of democracy, by the rhetoric of empowerment, and by the practice of participation. The evidence of the decline in respect for authority is everywhere—and everywhere are leaders who labor to lead. The change is cultural, contextual. Norms are now such that followers demand more—and leaders succumb more often.

Old World Order

Amy Vanderbilt's Complete Book of Etiquette, published in 1952, described the American family of its time as an orderly unit. Fathers had final authority, mothers ruled the roost when father was away, and children knew their place. To be sure, the husband was supposed to "consider himself a partner in the home, not its dictator," but it was clear he had final say. He was instructed, for example, to "give his wife some portion of their income, for her own use without any strings attached." So it was he who controlled the family purse and he who gave his wife an allowance, at his discretion, assuming he was "an agreeable husband." "The agreeable wife," in turn, was advised, among other things, to look the part. "A man's last glimpse of his wife in the morning and his first view of her at night"—after returning home from work—"should be pleasant experiences," Amy Vanderbilt wrote. Finally, children were expected, first and foremost, to behave, to exhibit good conduct in the presence of others. Mealtime, to take an obvious instance, was to be harmonious: the child "should be made to understand that meals with the rest of the family are a privilege, that no one member should make the others uncomfortable by bickering, noisy behavior, lounging all over the table, lack of grooming, etc."

Implied hierarchies—in this case, father at the top, mother in the middle, and children at the bottom—are in evidence throughout Vanderbilt's "guide to gracious living." They repeat themselves everywhere: in the ceremonies of life, in dress and in manners, in household management, and in the workplace. Proper relations between superiors and subordinates were the touchstone of everyday life, with women advised to "establish a dignified employer-employee relationship" with their "domestics," and to review their work "giving censure, encouragement, and praise as needed." Outside the home, men were similarly constrained. At the office the line between those lower down and those higher up was sharply drawn, the man being advised always to step "back to allow his superior to go first if the other is about to leave too, or, if there seems to be some delay, asks permission to go first."[1]

The workplace was, in fact, famously formal and famously, insufferably conforming. Sloan Wilson's 1955 bestselling novel, *The Man in the Gray Flannel Suit*, and William H. Whyte's 1956 bestselling study, *The Organization Man*, confirmed the increasingly obvious—that organizations had become behemoths and individual expression had been stifled. In the mid-1950s, eminent sociologist C. Wright Mills painted a broader picture, but the message was the same.[2] According to Mills, a cadre of political, economic, and military elites controlled a disproportionate amount of America's resources, including money and status, power and influence. Mills found that contrary to the myth of the American Dream, the United States was like everyplace else: it had an upper class that was dominant, and a playing field less level than was generally presumed. In other words, those who were down were likely to stay down, and those who were up were likely to remain in a position of privilege.

The literature on leadership and management back then was in keeping with the times—employers were at the top and employees in the middle or down below—which is why leadership scholarship focused on leadership traits. After all, no one else seemed much to matter. It was only the leader who had, or seemed to have, most of the power, all of the authority, and most of the influence. Researchers found that leaders were taller than their followers, more energetic and more assertive, and their speech was superior. Moreover, they were atypically intent on assuming responsibility, and particularly persistent in pursuit of their goals.[3] Put another way, leaders were different from their followers, who, to put it bluntly, were less excellent exemplars of the species.

No surprise then that in the 1950s and early '60s, leaders were generally thought of as being commanding and controlling. First they decided what was to be done and how. And then they declared their decision, without any obligation to provide any explanation. Participation by, or engagement of, followers was minimal, and complete compliance was expected.[4] Leadership scholar Joseph Rost called this the "industrial paradigm" of leadership. It was management oriented and goal dominated, authoritative and quantitative, short-term and cost-benefit driven, hierarchical and technical, rational, pragmatic, materialistic, and male.[5]

But, by the late 1950s, things began gradually to change, and the orderly world prescribed by Amy Vanderbilt was becoming ever so slightly disorderly. The idea that leaders could simply command and control and their will would be done gave way to the slow, sober realization that times were changing. Philip Selznick's classic 1957 book, *Leadership in Administration*, foreshadowed the future by debunking the idea that leaders were superior and therefore necessary, that leading was tantamount to exercising complete control, and that position was everything. What Selznick found instead was quite the opposite: that under certain circumstances leadership was "dispensable," that it necessarily involved others, and that it was "not equivalent to office-holding or high prestige or authority." In fact, Selznick concluded, leadership was associated more with persona than position.[6]

In a sign of the impending times, in February 1960 four young black men, apparently ordinary students at the Agricultural and Technical College of North Carolina, turned the world—at least our world, in the United States—upside down. They had the temerity to take a seat at a Woolworth's lunch counter in Greensboro, North Carolina, which clearly was marked Whites Only. A day later their protest was joined by twenty more, and four days after that their ranks had swelled to three hundred. In short order such sit-ins had spread throughout the South, with followers who were Participants,

Activists, and even Diehards hell-bent on changing the status quo, on bringing segregation to an end.

Less than a year after that came another pivotal moment in American history: the elderly, venerated five-star general who had been president for eight years, Dwight David Eisenhower, gave up the Oval Office to a young, handsome, Catholic upstart from Massachusetts, John Fitzgerald Kennedy. So, how to tell when a country is on the cusp of a time new and different? How to tell when change is significant, rather than merely routine? Surely those sit-ins in the South and the election of John F. Kennedy were harbingers of some sort, signs that the early 1960s divided the old from the new, the past from the present.

While change, even big change, is not generally signaled by the strike of a gong, it is no less real. Here then, again, is David Brooks: "I wonder if sometime around 50 years ago a great mental tide began to sweep across the world. Before the tide, people saw themselves in certain fixed places in the social order. They accepted opinions from trusted authorities. As the tide swept through, they began to see themselves differently. They felt they should express their own views, and these views deserved respect. They mentally bumped themselves up to first class and had a different set of expectations of how they should be treated."[7] In other words, for a constellation of reasons, "sometime around 50 years ago," the past gave way to a future in which followers "began to see themselves differently."

New World Order

During the late 1960s and early '70s, Samuel Huntington's American Creed resurfaced in a major way. Inspired by the ideals of the American Revolution—equality, liberty, individualism, and democracy—in the late 1960s, as in the late 1760s, the Creed created a culture not in keeping with, but contrary to conformity.

I have written elsewhere of this period under the heading "the world the sixties made," because for many Americans everyday life morphed during the late 1960s and early '70s into something else entirely.[8] While the targets of change varied—relations between blacks and whites, relations between women and men, the war in Vietnam—the result was always the same: a country and a culture more reminiscent of the one described a hundred years earlier by Tocqueville—in which there was a "general distaste for accepting any man's proof of anything"—than of America in the 1950s and the sedate, conformist "Eisenhower generation" that exemplified it.

As we have seen, in the late 1960s and early '70s, upheavals were everywhere. With the benefit of hindsight, it was a period from which leaders never fully recovered. They never again enjoyed their previous power and prestige, while followers never again were so trusting of people in positions of authority, or so willing to pay them due deference.

Judith Martin, who calls herself "Miss Manners" and is the best known of Amy Vanderbilt's several successors, has a conception of what constitutes "correct behavior" that is altogether different from what it was forty or fifty years ago. In contrast to Vanderbilt, Martin generally sides not with those higher up, but with those lower down. Now it is not so much children being told to behave as it is parents being informed that "rudeness to children counts as rudeness." Now the home is supposed to be anything but a model of well-ordered perfection: "To keep a house in which every object, down to the smallest bibelot, is in perfect taste is in shocking taste." And now parents, as opposed to being paragons of virtue in positions of authority, are advised explicitly to acknowledge their flaws and foibles, and to be communal rather than controlling. In the event of family discord, Martin writes, "An admission that you are all to blame, and you all also suffer from the resulting atmosphere, is the basis on which to suggest that you make a joint fresh start." Nor is the workplace exempt from this sort of rampant egalitarianism. For example, a woman who has been harassed by a superior should take on said superior, by every means necessary, including the law: "Resorting to the law should be the last resort, but you should give everyone involved a gentle reminder that it is available to you. . . . And you should keep saying it up the chain of command until you get to someone who . . . has the sense to get frightened."[9]

Once again, the leadership literature changed, reflecting the changing times. By the end of the twentieth century, leading by commanding and controlling was dead and gone, and leading by cooperating and collaborating was famously in fashion. Obviously this is all of a piece: the world the 1960s made had implications for patterns of dominance and deference in every sector of American society, including the burgeoning leadership industry.

It is important to note that though the shift was away from the leader and toward the follower, the leader never left center stage. In fact, the leader was distinguished from the ordinary "executive" and in particular from the "manager" by being described, certainly comparatively, as a more fabulous figure than ever. Warren Bennis was one among several prominent leadership experts who, beginning in the 1970s, differentiated the leader from the manager, invariably favoring the former, who was something of a swashbuckling hero, over the latter, who was a bureaucratic bore. Bennis described the leader as an innovator, whereas the manager was merely an administrator. Similarly, the leader was an "original," while the manager was just a "copy," and the leader inspired trust whereas the mere manager had to resort to control.[10] So it is not surprising that becoming a leader became a mantra—and it is not surprising that there was, that there still is, an apparently bottomless market for leadership training and development.

But even Bennis and like-minded colleagues now tempered their tone: they became inclusive instead of staying exclusive. By the turn of the century, no leadership course, text, or consultant would dare to teach how to be a leader without referring, if only sparingly and obliquely, to the follower. Bennis wrote about "getting people on your side," while words and terms such as *team*, *network*, *engagement*, *empowerment*, *cooperation*, *collaboration*, *participation*, and *flattened hierarchy* became touchstones in a time when power and authority were diminished, and influence necessarily was shared.

"Leadership," James Kouzes and Barry Posner wrote in their book, *The Leadership Challenge*, "is not a solo act, it's a team effort." The "ever increasing turbulence in the marketplace demands even more collaboration, not less."[11] Similarly, in his book, *Authentic Leadership*, Bill George concluded, "There is no doubt that CEOs have tremendous influence on the results of corporations. However if we examine more closely the success stories of the last twenty-five years . . . we see that each was built by a team at the top, not by a single person."[12] And in *Primal Leadership*, Daniel Goleman said the research proved "the superiority of group decision making over that of even the brightest individuals in the group."[13] In fact, Goleman went on to say that rather than leaders being aristocrats, they should now be democrats, "true collaborators" who work as "team members rather than top-down leaders." Great leaders, he wrote, are great listeners: they "create the sense that they truly want to hear employees' thoughts and concerns."[14]

Finally, to add insult to injury, by the first decade of the twenty-first century, leaders were being counseled to be, of all things, likable. So concerned must they be with what others might think, so vulnerable are they now to the slings and arrows of others, the pressure is on them to be, well, yes, nice. An article in *BusinessWeek* put it this way: "Senior executives seem to be battling for the congeniality prize. Humility, authenticity, and responsive leadership are the new buzzwords at the top. Many chief executives talk about being 'servant leaders' and team players. They care openly about everything from employees to Mother Earth. In short, they're more likable."[15]

We know that the old order is over because people in positions of power and authority seem similar to, as opposed to far more imposing than, those who are not; because they are routinely derided, ignored, or circumvented by those who are not, and because they find it increasingly difficult to exercise either the one (power) or the other (authority).

To a degree, the leadership industry does take into account this transformation in patterns of dominance and deference. In fact, a few experts have got to the point of concluding that leaders are dispensable altogether. (Ironically, if this were true, it would defeat the very purpose of the leadership industry.) "The absence of structure, leadership, and formal organization, once considered a weakness, has become a major asset," wrote Ori Brafman and Rod Beckstrom in *The Starfish and the Spider*.[16] But as a whole the industry is oblivious to history, to the fact that the assaults on power and authority that characterized the 1960s and '70s had effects that were enduring as well as contagious—threatening leadership cadres not only in the United States but, in time, nearly everywhere else.

Follower Power

Remember the name Monica Lewinsky? I mention her in this chapter about leadership and culture because nothing so strongly signaled the increasing empowerment of followers and the concomitant diminishment of leaders as the sex scandal that dominated American politics during the late 1990s. It enthralled the American people—while ensnaring their chief executive, President Bill Clinton, in a trap of his own making.

The point I make has nothing to do with whether the outrage against Clinton's sexual relationship with a White House intern was justified. Rather, I am addressing the stunningly unseemly national debate that was the result. It was a toxic mix: an intemperate president, an available young woman, a plethora of politicians excited by the smell of blood, a press corps with license to invade the most private parts of a president's personal life, and an insatiable public that felt no evident compunction about peeping at an unzipped president.

Rumors about Bill Clinton's womanizing had permeated his political career, and his sex life was front-page news even during his first presidential campaign. Still, no one really thought his errant ways would persist into the White House. No one really imagined his sexual relationship with one Monica Lewinsky would one day result in his impeachment, impede his presidency, and end in a sordid national soap opera.

The Lewinsky affair came to light as the result of an earlier charge of sexual harassment, which ultimately exposed the president to public scrutiny in a way aptly described by Clinton biographer John Harris as "grotesquely literal."[17] Moreover, once the story became a scandal and the president was finally obliged to respond publicly, the drama was further heightened and the president further humiliated. Ultimately Clinton admitted that he had had a relationship with Lewinsky that was "inappropriate," and he apologized. But the damage was done—and the story became a cross between a national joke and a national embarrassment.

But Bill Clinton hasn't been the only recent leader subjected to this sort of ritualistic debasement. In fact, the list of leaders in similar situations is surprisingly long, well-known names in American business as well as government, including Harry Stonecipher, Mark Hurd, Eliot Spitzer, Mark Sanford, and Anthony Weiner. Stonecipher was forced by the board of Boeing to resign as CEO after it learned he had a romantic relationship with a female employee. Hurd was obliged to resign as CEO of Hewlett-Packard after a sexual harassment probe revealed he had personal ties to a female contractor, who had also received from him "inappropriate payments." Spitzer was compelled to quit as governor of New York when the *New York Times* disclosed he regularly patronized a prostitution service. Mark Sanford did manage to finish his term as governor of South Carolina, but the scandal that erupted when he went missing for six days to pay his "soul mate" in Argentina a clandestine visit cost him dearly. He was censured for misuse of government funds and obliged to surrender his chairmanship of the Republican Governors Association. And Representative Anthony Weiner—who, after tweeting lewd pictures of himself, became the butt of a billion jokes—was veritably forced to step down from the political stage after being hounded by even those in his own party.

Obviously in this day and age followers feel entitled to pry into their leaders' private lives—and to hold them accountable for what they do. When John Kennedy was in the White House, the American people had no idea that he was a reckless and tireless bounder. When Franklin Roosevelt was in the White House, the American people had no idea that he was essentially paralyzed and confined to a wheelchair. And when Woodrow Wilson was in the White House, the American people had no idea that he was so severely disabled by a stroke that during the last eighteen months of his presidency, his wife, Edith Bolling Galt Wilson, in effect governed the country.

Of course, now is hardly the first time in human history that men in positions of power and authority had sexual relations with women other than their wives; nor is now the first time in human history that people in positions of power and authority have in some way been impaired. But it is the first time in human history that information has been democratized—that we all have nearly unbridled and instantaneous access to information about even the ostensibly high and mighty. And it is the first time the culture is such that censure for prurient invasions of privacy is, largely, absent. The Oprahization of American culture is the jewel in this crown—we think we have an absolute right to know everything there is to know about anyone who is a person of interest.

The impact of these regular invasions into the lives of leaders is impossible to calculate precisely. What we do know though is this: they diminish and demean leaders and elevate and embolden followers. When everyone is exposed to the point of being vulnerable—no matter their status or station—the gap between leaders and followers shrinks to near the vanishing point. As a result, the conversation has been coarsened. "Here's the thing . . . the president is full of crap!" opined popular cable news anchor Keith Olbermann, referring to George W. Bush, in 2008. Barack Obama is a "dick," suggested esteemed journalist Mark Halperin, live and on the air, in 2011. As a result, the power and influence of leaders, of people in positions of authority, have been diminished, while the power and influence of followers, of ordinary people, has been enhanced.

Incidentally, the evidence of this leveling is everywhere, including in the popular culture. In times past no one much cared what you thought, or what I thought, about anything. We didn't much count, nor did our opinions, especially not on subjects about which we knew absolutely nothing. Experts, people with authority and credibility, were considered to have the requisite knowledge and experience to weigh in—and so they did. They were the ones who dictated what was good and what was bad, while we in turn deferred. That was then.

This is now, when everyday life is the rough equivalent of *American Idol* or *Dancing with the Stars*. The winners of these immensely popular televised talent shows are decided not by the experts, men and women who are singers or dancers themselves, or have some relevant experience or expertise. The experts are part of the proceedings—they select the talent that competes, and they critique the contestants' performances—but we are the ones with final say. The winners are decided by you and me, by ordinary people who telephone or text or use some other technology to cast their vote to determine the outcomes.

Participatory democracy of this kind is now everywhere in evidence. Everywhere we weigh in, register our opinion, and express our preferences, needs, wants, and wishes. Sometimes the effect of this engagement is entirely symbolic; sometimes the effect is real, of consequence. It is in any case the act of self-expression itself that matters. It further fuels our sense of entitlement and empowerment, and it further devalues those better schooled or credentialed, more informed than we.

Once upon a time there was no such thing as a focus group or crowdsourcing. Now they are ubiquitous, groups of ordinary people whose opinions and attitudes are for various reasons considered significant. For example, focus groups in marketing have become important tools for soliciting feedback on products. Focus groups in organizations have become important tools for planning and evaluation. And focus groups in politics have become important sources of information on voter preferences, both on policies and on the politicians who proselytize on their behalf. In other words, in such circumstances, it is focus groups—followers, not leaders—who are driving the action. Crowdsourcing is in some ways similar, a follower phenomenon in its own right, in which ordinary people assemble, virtually, not literally, to accomplish a particular task or serve a particular purpose. For example, PepsiCo's Pepsi Refresh Project, which gives grants to "generate innovative, optimistic ideas," such as improving parks and playgrounds, describes itself as a crowdsourcing movement using various social platforms, including Facebook and Twitter.

It used to be there was no such thing as 360-degree feedback, which asks subordinates, among others, to assess their superiors on a range of traits, skills, and capacities previously considered beyond the purview of those below. Nor for that matter was there such a thing as "upward feedback," the sole purpose of which is to have leaders and managers critiqued and evaluated by those who report to them.

Similarly, a half century ago, how many teachers were assessed, in every course, by their students? Nearly none. Now student evaluations are part of the process, a regular ritual to those familiar with the inside of a college and, yes, even a high school classroom. At the Harvard Kennedy School, where I have taught for over a decade, at the end of every semester students rate every one of their courses—and every one of their professors. Whatever the rigor of the evaluations, the point is that in institutions of higher and secondary education, subordinates regularly judge their superiors—with consequences that can be considerable. For even at the college level, many institutions now promote faculty and award tenure not only on the basis of their scholarship, but also on the basis of their teaching, which was assessed primarily if not exclusively by those being taught.

Then there are sources like Zagat's, Yelp, CitySearch, and TripAdvisor—further indicators of follower power, of people power. Zagat pioneered the trend: it started in 1979 to collect ratings of restaurants not by the usual experts, but by diners like you and me, who suddenly were somehow empowered to weigh in on what constitutes a good restaurant experience and what does not. Since then, it and other similar, now largely online sites (Zagat itself has been sold to Google) have become ubiquitous, soliciting opinions from ordinary people on a whole range of their experiences—hotels, shopping, travel, you name it—creating yet another situation in which the many expect to be heard, not only a select few.

This brings us finally to polls—those countless, relentless surveys that ask people everywhere for their opinions about everything and everyone. Our incessant need to know what ordinary people around the world think and believe and like and dislike is indicative of the cumulative impact of followers on leaders purportedly in charge.

Leader Limits

The converse of follower power, its necessary corollary, is leader limits: formal and informal limits, political limits, professional limits, and personal limits. There are limits on leaders' capacity to wield power, exercise authority, and exert influence. And there are other sorts of limits as well, such as leaders' ability to maintain a zone of privacy, arbitrarily extend their tenure as executives, and protect themselves against the slanders of others. The only leader who is entirely free of such limits is the tyrannical leader—the leader who is willing and able to use power to coerce.

To be sure, though leaders are constrained now by the culture within which they operate, and by followers who feel freer than before to demean and debase those at the top, bad leaders remain ubiquitous. But when followers know full well that their leader has fallen short, and when enough of them happen really to care, and when, to boot, they have a modicum of freedom, leaders are newly vulnerable. Simple case in point: New York City mayor Michael Bloomberg, who in spite of his being generally admired, and in spite of his having secured for himself an exceptional (and previously illegal) third term, was nevertheless humbled—by the weather. In December 2010, New York was hit by a blizzard that overwhelmed the city with heavy snow and ice and frigid temperatures. New Yorkers expected their streets to remain passable at all times, at least for emergency vehicles. What they got instead was too little too late, days of plows postponed. Their response was predictable—rage and outrage so extreme, the incident threatened permanently to tarnish Bloomberg's long-standing and well-burnished reputation for being clever and competent.

Complaints about the mayor's performance began pouring in soon after the last flake fell—by phone, email, fax, and Facebook, you name it, followers from incredulous to furious exercising their freedom of speech. Nor was the situation helped by what was, at least initially, the mayor's arrogant attitude—his telling beleaguered New Yorkers that the sixth-largest storm in city history was merely "inconvenient," and insisting his administration was "doing exactly what you'd expect it to do."

Having been chastised and chastened—Brooklyn's borough president told the mayor the city had "handled this horribly"—Bloomberg, ordinarily the least modest of public servants, ate crow. He apologized repeatedly for his administration's ineptitude and assured anyone and everyone that each and every street would be plowed and each and every vehicle pushed or pulled from the frozen muck and mire. The mayor acknowledged that his administration had failed to adequately respond to the crisis and promised that it would never happen again—which, for the rest of that atypically cold and snowy winter, it did not.[18] Moreover, when less than a year later Hurricane Irene hit, Bloomberg's response was so inordinately vigorous, it was thought by many to be extreme.

But by no means are leaders vulnerable only when their failures are obvious, egregious, and of immediate consequence. Twenty-first-century leaders must prepare to be pushed from their perch even when things are going generally well, even when they've committed no grievous error, never mind cardinal sin, even when there's no clear and present reason to send them packing.

Consider the case of Lawrence Summers, who in 2001 became president of Harvard University. Though Summers was never particularly popular with Harvard faculty, during his first few years in office he led the school with competence and intelligence, including planning for an ambitious campus expansion and a revision of the undergraduate curriculum. However, the minute he made a major political mistake by suggesting there might be "intrinsic" reasons why women were less successful in science and engineering than men, members of the faculty—not all, but some, enough—became outraged to the point of rebellion.

During the next year faculty—again, not all, but some, enough—became increasingly embittered and emboldened, attacking Summers loudly and often, and questioning his fitness to be president. Finally there was a faculty vote of no confidence in Summers that was in no way binding—but it was a historic first. Never before in Harvard's long and storied history had faculty sent such a message or so personally and professionally humiliated a sitting president. Things came to a head in 2006, at yet another faculty meeting dominated by the subject of Summers. Fifteen members came out against him; no one, at least on that occasion, spoke in his defense. A second vote of no confidence was threatened—which persuaded the president he had to resign. In a letter to the Harvard community

Summers acknowledged that his tenure had been marked by "strains and moments of rancor," and that the divisions between him and the faculty had finally made it "infeasible" for him to continue to lead.

Nor was Summers the only university president in recent years to have been tarred and feathered—as Bob Kerrey, former governor and senator from Nebraska, then president of the New School, could be the first to attest. Kerrey was among the most admired of the nation's public officials when he was named president of the prestigious New School in 2001. Charged by the board with creating major change, Kerrey proceeded to do just that—he was able to increase applications and enrollment and grow the endowment. But, similar to Summers, his constituents, his ostensible followers, just didn't like him. They considered him disrespectful of the academic culture and guilty of what they judged his high-handed management style. In time students protested and members of the faculty joined to censure their president with a vote of no confidence. They charged Kerrey with having made it "virtually impossible for the faculty to be properly involved in thoughtful and effective academic planning."[19] He toughed it out and hung on for a time, but his tenure had been irrevocably marred and he felt obliged ultimately to resign.

As always, patterns of dominance and deference tend over time to converge. So whatever the trend in one area, it is likely eventually to affect leaders and followers in another. In 2010, Harvard Business Press published a book by Vineet Nayar titled *Employees First, Customers Second*. The book proposes a shift away from traditional management systems in which the leader is at the center, to new sorts of systems, in which organizations are self-run and self-governed.

Interestingly, like Amy Vanderbilt and Judith Martin (and for that matter, Sigmund Freud), Nayar writes about the family—

about how habits developed early in life persist. He points out that in traditional families "parents were the ultimate authorities" and children did as they were told or they were punished. But he, like Martin, suggests that families now are different from before. Now parents want to be friends and mentors to their children—not authority figures. So, similarly, organizations are different now from what they were not long ago. Because of the "knowledge economy" and changes in the "global IT landscape," it is critical, claims Nayar, that organizational structures, like the family structures they are said to mirror, adapt to the changing times. How? By having the CEO recede from foreground into background, to a point where he or she is more of a coach, a facilitator, or a genial host at a family gathering than a lodestar around whom turns everything and everyone.[20]

This is the arc of history—recent incarnations of the devolution of power and influence and the diminishment of authority. We are reminded that context—in this case culture—is as important to patterns of dominance and deference as are leaders and followers. And we are primed for the technological imperatives that further explain change.

3

Technological Imperatives—
losing control

In the mid- to late eighteenth century it was newspapers that sustained the American insurgency. They persuaded colonial readers of their personal stake in political protests against the English crown.[1] There were, of course, other channels of communication as well—learned pamphlets, for example, and committees of various sorts, which facilitated conversations face-to-face. But newspapers were an early iteration of a communication technology with consequences. They facilitated the shared ideas and information that finally fueled the revolution. It was the combustible mix— of information, expression, and connection—that led to action, to changing the balance between leaders and followers, then as it does now.

Information

We now know that along with everything else, leadership changes. But in the last thirty, forty years changes in leadership and followership have been the result of two phenomena in particular: the first is cultural change and the second is technological change, advances in communications technologies that led to more information, greater self-expression, and expanded connection.

Though once he was eminent, the late Harlan Cleveland is now largely forgotten. He had an illustrious career as a diplomat, educator, and, toward the end of his life, as an author. In 1997 he penned a pamphlet titled *Leadership and the Information Revolution*, in which, with precision and prescience, he identified, as no one else had, how information dissemination would affect leadership and followership.

Years before cell phones became ubiquitous, and light-years before the likes of Facebook and Twitter, Cleveland realized that information was a game changer. Unlike other resources, information expands as it is used, and it leaks. Moreover it is shared, not exchanged, and once it's been shared, disseminated, and diffused, it has the potential for significant impact. As Cleveland pointed out, the spread of information, at the time through television and copiers, was responsible for the "people power" that changed history—beginning in 1989.[2]

Cleveland's reference was, of course, to the iconic, symbolic fall of the Berlin Wall and to the collapse of communism in the Soviet Union and East Europe. He understood the impact of "information systems" not only on those with power and authority but, more to the point, on those without. He understood the ways in which information and technology tandem, to empower people who previously had neither. Even then, this applied particularly to young people, who knew better than their elders how to use new tools newly at their disposal. Nearly a decade and a half before the revolutions in Tunisia and Egypt, Cleveland wrote this: "The tidal waves of social change in my lifetime—environmental sensitivity, civil rights for all races, the enhanced status of women . . . were *not* generated by established leaders in government, business, religion, or even higher education. They boiled up from the people, with the help of new, often younger, leaders who had not previously been heard from."[3]

The trend continues. Advances in communications technologies make information instant and, of course, available to nearly everyone everywhere: information is sent one to one (email), one to many (home page, blog, Twitter), many to one (Wikipedia), and many to many (social networking sites).[4] The effect on leaders is, once again, to diminish them. We have already seen that people in positions of power are easily weakened by disclosures of personal information. Now we see that they are easily weakened by disclosures of professional information. The more we know about how leaders lead and managers manage, the more they tend to shrink. They are revealed, naked as it were, emperors without clothes, while we stand and stare, no longer surprised to find that they, like we, are merely mortal.

Take Julian Assange, a twenty-first century Australian anarchist, who, so far as disclosure and dissemination of information are concerned, broke nearly every rule in the book. Assange, the man behind WikiLeaks, is an odd, bold, arrogant, and impertinent transnational activist, to whom radical transparency is the Holy Grail. His medium is sometimes but by no means always in collaboration with mainstream media. And his message is: upend traditional journalism, bleed the culture of secrecy, give ordinary people access to information withheld, and press those in positions of power and authority to adopt policies and procedures in keeping with new norms of legitimacy and justice.

In 2010, WikiLeaks started posting items from a cache of 251,287 formerly secret U.S. diplomatic cables. Whatever the specific intentions behind the "dump" of documents, as they related to, for example, the war in Afghanistan, there was a general purpose as well: "to open up the inner workings of a closed and complex system, to call the world in to help judge its morality."[5] It is precisely this notion—the idea that ordinary people use unbridled access to information to judge those who are more elevated—that is nothing short of revolutionary.

The impact of WikiLeaks and analogous intrusions on secrecy in government and business is, obviously, impossible to assess precisely. In fact, one could claim the leaks themselves change little—note the continuing albeit somewhat reduced American presence in Afghanistan. Still, at a minimum they diminish those in charge—a position that even the following few leaks would seem to support: we now know that the war in Afghanistan has all along gone less well than the administrations of both Presidents George W. Bush and Barack Obama were willing publicly to admit; we now know that the war in Iraq was fought to an unprecedented degree by private contractors—who wore no uniforms, had few rules of engagement, and were subject to lax oversight; and we now know that whatever the public posturing, privately Iran has been the object of fear and loathing by several of its Arab neighbors, who secretly pleaded with the United States to attack Tehran's nuclear program.

Nor is the private sector immune from public prying. For example, Assange threatened to "take down" at least one major American bank by disclosing its unsavory secrets. In response to his charge of an "ecosystem of corruption"—of which Assange claimed there was proof—Bank of America, which feared it was the target, played defense. As reported by the *New York Times*, fifteen to twenty Bank of America officials conducted an extensive internal investigation, scouring thousands of documents in the event there was an attempt to make them public.[6] Similarly, WikiLeaks released information that embarrassed Royal Dutch Shell. As described by the *Wall Street Journal*, Shell executives had been "dismissive" of the Nigerian officials with whom they did business, and "nervous about the pending changes in the nation's oil industry." So, to keep tabs on a Nigerian government that Shell considered inept and altogether too eager to do business with China and Russia, the company secretly placed its own personnel in "all relevant [Nigerian] ministries."[7]

Of course, some leaks are purely petty, the stuff of diplomatic gossip. But other leaks, leaks other than those from WikiLeaks, have been the sole source of information intended to humiliate, irritate, or infuriate people in positions of power and authority. In San Diego, a handful of young journalists created a website (VoiceofSanDiego.org) that exposed some of the city's darkest secrets. City officials with conflicts of interest and hidden pay raises, supposedly affordable housing that was unaffordable, misleading crime statistics.[8] In France, charges of illegal financial donations involving officials at the highest levels of government, up to and including President Nicolas Sarkozy, were stoked by a news website called Mediapart. And in the Middle East, documents were leaked to Al Jazeera that revealed that in spite of their long-standing public protests against the construction of Jewish developments in contested areas, Palestinian negotiators had been secretly willing to cede to Israel large tracts of Jerusalem. (Al Jazeera's revelations triggered an outpouring of anger at leaders of the Palestinian Authority, which held uncompromising positions in public but appeared "to have given way to Israel in private.")[9]

So how exactly does the spread of information weaken leaders? Even this quick account suggests the following degradations: leaders are exposed as liars, as duplicitous; leaders are exposed as weak, foolish, and inept; leaders are exposed as intemperate and corrupt; and leaders are derailed by overt disclosures of covert plans. To this list one might reasonably respond by asking, so what's new? Who in this day and age is surprised by the fact that leaders lie and cheat and steal? Not many. Still, the regular drumbeat of information about leaders behaving badly can be dispiriting, and it emboldens followers who, smelling blood, attack.

Putting the genie back in the bottle, stopping the flow of information, is of course impossible, which some find aggravating to the point of infuriating. Though online leaks are credited with important contributions—for example, to the exercise of people power in Tunisia—they are also often the object of blame, for instance, for endangering Morgan Tsvangirai, prime minister of Zimbabwe and leader of the democratic opposition to its despotic president, Robert Mugabe.[10] Assange has, in any case, become a whipping boy for a whole host of leaders, from President Barack Obama, whose secretary of state, Hillary Clinton, charged that WikiLeaks put people's lives in jeopardy, to Colonel Muammar Gaddafi, who, while still in power, was incensed by being no longer able to hoard that which previously was his private reserve—information. Additionally, WikiLeaks is in trouble, in danger of being shut down by the blockade on donations imposed by financial service companies such as Visa and MasterCard. Even more telling was what happened to Bradley Manning, the American soldier charged by the U.S. government with having turned over to WikiLeaks huge amounts of classified documents. Manning, in his early twenties, was held in solitary confinement from July 2010 to April 2011, when he finally was transferred, probably because of growing public outrage over the severity of his treatment, to a medium-security facility. Of course there are a good number who take the opposite view of WikiLeaks—to them, to supporters of radical transparency, Assange is a hero.

In the end, of course, it does not much matter what I think or what you think or what anyone thinks, no matter how highly positioned or how much of an expert. It is what it is. To be sure, efforts to constrain the dissemination of information continue nonstop. Authoritarian governments such as those in Iran, China, and North Korea censor the Web and crack down on bloggers and do whatever else they can to cut the conversation. In fact, the Iranian government is attempting to disconnect Iranian cyberspace from the rest of the Web, thereby confining their people to their own, internal, network. Still, the flow of information is impossible completely to stanch, and its spread is impossible completely to stop. This applies to information that for present purposes can be labeled "objective"— that is, ostensibly factual information obtained from ostensibly independent sources. And it applies to information that for present purposes can be labeled "subjective"—that is, personal information about who we are and how we feel. It is to this second type of information—expression—to which I now turn.

Expression

"Freedom of expression" is considered a cornerstone of democracy and human rights. It presumes political liberty—people ought to be free to say what they want, when they want, and where they want, so long as it is not falsely crying fire in a crowded theater. But in the twenty-first century, freedom of expression has another definition: freedom to say anything to anyone about anything or anyone, anywhere, at any time, in real time.

The impact of what is said, typed, texted, or depicted depends, of course, on who exactly is paying attention—on who are your listeners, viewers, readers, "friends," and "followers." Still, quantity can be less important than quality: the act of self-expression, of saying what we want when we want, is what matters. The number of people who are wired is now so humongous that we simply assume that at least one person somewhere is paying attention—which is why having our say seems important.

In 2012 the number of Facebook users is expected to reach one billion worldwide. By and large Facebook is used for purposes best described as utterly ordinary—we use it to express ourselves about ordinary things in ordinary ways. We share who we are and what we want, what we did and how we did it, and what we think and feel. Facebook is about providing information and about making a connection and about establishing community—but above all it is about personal expression, providing a medium for everyone who wants and has access to post presentations of self. Notwithstanding periodic protests against Facebook for invasions of privacy, it overwhelmingly testifies to the apparently considerable pleasures of being known.

Twitter, because of its brevity (each tweet is no more than 140 characters), is more even than Facebook about instant gratification. But, like Facebook, what has turned out so striking is not only Twitter's speed but its range—its communication of content ranging from the totally trivial to the utterly consequential. Among several other reasons, Twitter is so extremely quick and easy or, as media critic David Carr put it, "The act of publishing on Twitter is so friction-free—a few keystrokes and hit send—that you can forget that others are out there listening."[11]

Think of it as an evolution in our understanding of the content of which Twitter, Facebook, and other social media are capable. For instance, we've reached a point where customers (that is, followers) tweeting in consequential numbers can oblige companies (that is, leaders and managers) to respond, in effect, from one moment to the next. As soon as someone noticed, and posted, that Amazon had reclassified books with gay and lesbian themes as "adult"—thereby removing them from certain search and sales rankings—protests erupted. Where? In the blogosphere, of course, and on Twitter, compelling the company immediately to correct the situation, in spite of it being the Easter holiday. Similarly, when Kenneth Cole, a leader in the fashion industry and a regular tweeter, apparently went beyond the pale by seeming to make light of the Egyptian Revolution, he was blasted, accused of being tacky, greedy, and politically insensitive. His response was within the hour—he backtracked and apologized, profusely, first on Twitter and then on Facebook. As Cole put it to Tavis Smiley some weeks later, he learned to his chagrin that "everyone is empowered." And when the CEO of Netflix, Reed Hastings, faced a precipitous decline in the company's stock price as a result of tens of thousands of online protests against his 60 percent price hike and decision to split the company, he ate humble pie. He reversed himself on the split and he apologized. "I messed up," Hastings wrote to his customers. "I owe you an explanation."[12] (Hastings's mea culpa did not help. His company ended the third quarter of 2011 with fully 800,000 fewer subscribers in the United States than in the previous quarter. Nor was a lesson learned. Just a few months later, Verizon Wireless felt compelled, after one day of consumer vitriol flooding the Web, to reverse its plan to impose a two-dollar bill-paying fee.)

Corporate America's response to the power and peril of social networking has been to spend—in particular to bring in people who can serve as "social media managers." Petco, Panasonic, Citigroup, and AT&T are just a few of the many companies that have hired (or intend to) such managers, tasked with responding to, that is, mollifying, ordinary people, with freedom of expression and the technological capacity to exercise it morning, noon, and night.

But however important social media are to people in positions of power and authority in business, recent history suggests they are more important to people in positions of power and authority in government. The courts have been affected, with judges compelled to call a mistrial when, contrary to instructions, jurors use electronic devices to pass on information or give an opinion bearing on a case.[13] Politics have been affected, from politicians who were nearly entirely unknown becoming president to constituents voicing their opinions more loudly and stridently than previously. And world affairs have been affected. Sometimes the effect seems relatively small: two weeks after the U.S. State Department helped set up a social network in Pakistan, more than a million text messages were sent. But sometimes the effect of social media on world affairs is huge, nearly overwhelming: to wit the Egyptian Revolution. What has in any case become clear is that people who use social media to express themselves on minor matters are, if the occasion arises, ready, willing, and able to use social media to express themselves on major matters—on matters of significance such as governance.

Months before any of the eruptions in the Middle East, an op-ed appeared in the *New York Times* titled "When Arabs Tweet." Writer Rami Khouri pointed to a "continuing social revolution in how youth throughout the Middle East use Web sites, cell phones, chat systems, blogs, Twitter, Facebook and other rapidly evolving new media." Though at the time these young people were connecting mainly for mundane reasons, such as promoting a new movie or arranging a dance party, the important thing was that they were getting in the habit of expressing themselves, first finding their voice, then finding someone somewhere was listening.[14]

It is impossible to talk about change, so far as leadership and followership are concerned, without talking simultaneously about generational change. This was strikingly in evidence in the Middle East, where the Arab Spring was initiated and inspired by the young and restless, not the old and entrenched, or even by the middle-aged. This is a domestic phenomenon as well, as prevalent in the United States as it is elsewhere in the world. Tammy Erickson has written extensively about Gen X'ers, Americans born in the 1960s and '70s, who, she found, differ from their elders, particularly with regard to patterns of dominance and deference. Gen X'ers are, in comparison with those a generation or two older, more distrustful of individuals and institutions, more comfortable in the global and digital world, more self-reliant and outward looking, and more en-trepreneurial, inclined to "look for a different way forward."[5] They are also more likely than their immediate predecessors to challenge authority, indirectly, through social media, if not directly, and even less likely than their immediate predecessors to play the part of passive follower or to adapt easily to traditional hierarchies. All this applies the more to Gen Y'ers (Net Geners, Millennials), born in the 1980s and '90s.

We begin to see the sequence: new technologies enable the dissemination of information; in turn social media enable the expression the information engenders. Thus bad leaders are quite right to fear freedom of expression. For once we express what we think and feel, we tend to think and feel it the more fervently. In turn, in the event our fervor is well founded, it is likely as not in the time of Twitter to be picked up by others, experienced by others, emulated by others. Moreover expression empowers—followers have their say and in so saying they are emboldened. As more than a hundred thousand people joined a Facebook page established in memory of twenty-eight-year-old Egyptian computer programmer Khaled Said to express their anger at his brutal killing by police, the effect was contagious and individual rage was transformed into a social move-ment. And what happened in Egypt happened later on, to vary-ing degrees, in a slew of other countries, including Syria, Jordan, Yemen, Libya, and Bahrain.

Connection

More questions: If a tree falls in a forest and no one is there to hear, does it make a sound? If you tweet but have no followers, do your messages matter? Can something exist without being perceived?

It's one thing to have media that enable the spread of information, and another to have media that enable self-expression. But these are acts in isolation—both spreading information and self-expressing can be accomplished alone, neither requiring the involvement of anyone else. This is why *social* media tools, such as text messaging, email, photo sharing, and social networking, are something else entirely. What sets social media apart from other media is that they are designed to facilitate interpersonal engagement, sometimes one to one, sometimes in groups.

Which brings me back to this: by and large the land of connection is the land of the young. It is they who are tech savvy, who venture into and become familiar with the latest in social media, typically in ways and to a degree that leave their elders in the dust. As the U.S. chief of naval operations, Admiral Gary Roughead, put it, "For whether we [leaders] embrace the fundamental communications changes under way today or not, our talented young workforce not only embraces them, they know nothing else."[16] The fact is that leaders and managers worldwide, in both business and government, have been stunningly slow to get with the program. There are, of course, a few who signed on early. In corporate America, for instance, Alan Mulally at Ford, Tony Hsieh at Zappos, and Howard Schultz at Starbucks all embraced social media, and their companies in turn all benefited. But they are the exceptions.[17]

As recently as late 2010, 64 percent of American CEOs were not using social media of any kind for the purpose of connecting to their boards, employees, and customers, or for that matter to the public at large. This is not to say that CEOs don't reach out—they do. But the large majority of them continue to do so in ways that are decidedly old-fashioned, by being quoted in the news or by speaking directly to different audiences at different events. This leaves only about a third of CEOs who engage with their stakeholders, their followers, by employing technologies such as their own corporate websites, podcasts, blogs, or YouTube channels, or through social networks such as Facebook, Twitter, and LinkedIn.[18]

Why this should be so is a matter of conjecture, though age, habit, hubris, and leaders' overweening need to control (impossible on the Internet) all likely play a part. Their loss—for the early evidence suggests that CEOs who are connected have a considerable advantage. The most admired CEOs have an online presence, and the most successful companies have leaders and managers who know a little something about connecting and community building.[19] As one observer noted, given the risks and the time involved it's not surprising that so few CEOs choose not to engage in two-way conversations. But what is surprising is that so few CEOs are using social media to engage with others in their companies, to share information and ideas from their companies' perspective, and to empower their workforce to communicate on behalf of the organization. Put bluntly, they are committing what Roughead referred to as "a strategic error of the most basic nature."[20] They are wasting the opportunity to lead and manage in cyberspace.[21]

Of course, the risk to leaders and managers who are ignorant in the ways of new media is generally greater in government than in business, simply because the stakes are higher. Think of what transpired in Tunisia and Egypt in recent years, beneath the radar, or at least beneath the prying eyes of those in positions of power. The young connected to plot and plan while their elders remained oblivious. In particular, pan-Arab activists, nearly all of them young, were on Facebook years before the revolutions actually took place. They were busy brainstorming early on about everything from employing technology to evading surveillance, to organizing barricades. Once they were joined more openly with others, such as Egyptian activist Wael Ghonim, a thirty-one-year-old Google executive, their capacity for connecting to larger audiences increased exponentially. As the *New York Times* reported, the Facebook page that Ghonim set up in tribute to Khaled Said "eventually attracted hundreds of thousands of users, building their allegiance through exercises in online democratic participation."[22]

The Internet, and social media in particular, played a similar role in creating change in China—which is no longer totalitarian or even communist as conventionally conceived. As a result of online information, expression, and connection, China's leaders, eager as they were for rapid economic development, had no choice but to be at least slightly open. As Guobin Yang put it in *The Power of the Internet in China*, people in China are no longer "captive audiences." Rather they are "skilled actors" in a complex media environment. Thus "political domination shapes the forms of contention but cannot prevent it from happening."[23]

China is singular in that it combines political repression with high levels of educational and economic development. So though online activists in China are in some ways similar to online activists elsewhere—they tend to live in cities and to be young and well educated—they are in other ways different. They obviously have far less freedom of expression, and they are far more vulnerable to repression and even prosecution. Nevertheless, online activism in China has persisted, occasionally even amounting to a sustained political campaign, "with legitimate and independent organizational bases."[24] This raises a familiar and more general question: Does economic growth depend on freedom and democracy? Or can it take place without them?

To some it seems that China has found a third way—market authoritarianism, it's been called—a way of commingling a relatively high degree of economic growth with a relatively high degree of political repression. Perhaps—but the level of activism in China during the last decade or so, online and otherwise, suggests a more nuanced picture. For most of the twenty-first century, repression in China, however intermittently virulent, has gone only so far—because there was no real zeal to go any further. Even by now China is too highly developed and technologically sophisticated for political repression to be free of repercussion. So leaders in China, both political and corporate, are likely to continue for some time their balancing act: a passion for political order on the one hand, and a passion for economic development on the other.

Action

The Internet is obviously having an impact on relations between leaders and followers in the United States as well as in China. What is less clear is the nature of this impact. On the one side are the detractors, those like Malcolm Gladwell, who argue that social networks are effective at increasing participation, precisely by *lessening* the level of motivation required by online engagement. In an article that, in retrospect, is embarrassingly wrongheaded—it was published shortly *before* the revolutions in Tunisia and Egypt—Gladwell wrote that online activism "makes it easier for activists to express themselves, and harder for that expression to have any impact."[25] On the other side are those like Clay Shirky, who insist, generally correctly, that though decentralized technologies do not have a single preordained outcome, they have in fact become coordinating tools for "nearly all of the world's political movements" and they are nearly everywhere enabling new kinds of cooperative structures, for example in business, science, and the arts.[26]

Similarly, there is debate about the virtues of the wired world. In his book, *The Net Delusion*, Evgeny Morozov argues that the Internet, rather than promoting freedom, often restricts it.[27] In Iran the authorities have learned how to use online information to track down their opponents; and in China and Russia the government co-opts or pays bloggers to spread comments favorable to the state. The private sector provides a parallel: employers generally retain the right to monitor computers used by employees, who in turn must be more careful than before in case they are watched.

Of course, once again countless others take the opposite view: they tout the blessings of digital democracy, its leveling effect, its transparency and connectivity, its high rate of participation by low-level players, and the medium it provides for upending people in positions of authority. Though he is cautious about whether Internet use will, in the end, really make political liberation more likely, seasoned journalist Steve Coll has made clear his opinion, which is mine as well, that social media played a significant part in both the Tunisian and Egyptian revolutions, as well as in the political turmoil that soon spread to other Arab and Muslim nations.[28] Of course, they also played a part in the 2011 street riots in London, the worst in a generation, prompting Prime Minister David Cameron to tell Parliament (foolishly) that his government was exploring ways of banning people from social networking sites if they were thought to be planning criminal activity. And of course social media also played a part in Occupy Wall Street, a series of protests that started small and local and, within weeks, went large and global.

Despite disagreement over the level of its impact, as well as over its merits and deficits, it is inarguable that the Internet engages

millions of people in collective conversations that before would
have been impossible. In the process it diffuses and disseminates
resources previously available to only an elite few—first information and then influence.

According to a 2010 study by the Pew Research Center's Internet
& American Life Project, about 25 million Americans are "online
political activists." How are such activists defined? According to
Pew, they are engaged *every single day* in sifting the news, sharing
concerns, and attempting to shift the debate.[29] They are, in short,
not merely Participants in the political process, but Activists, followers who feel strongly about their leaders, pro or con, and act accordingly.[30]

This heightened sense of entitlement—of being entitled to participate is a worldwide phenomenon. In China, text messaging
and video uploading enabled workers at a Honda Lock auto parts
factory to, in effect, go on strike. First, 1,700 workers left their
workstations. Then, several hours later, they posted an account of
their walkout online, spreading the word not only to each other but
also to restive workers elsewhere in China. Next they fired off cell
phone text messages urging colleagues to resist pressure from factory bosses, and finally they logged onto a state-controlled website
that was a digital hub of the Chinese labor movement. Armed with
desktop computers, they uploaded various videos, including some
that showed Honda Lock's security guards roughing up employees.[31]
Along similar lines, in Russia videos detailing police corruption—
payoffs, extortion, and illegal arrests—were watched more than two
million times, causing a sensation and stirring a national debate
as well as widespread public outrage. The hue and cry resulted in
a rare public admission: President Dmitri Medvedev conceded that
police corruption constituted a major problem.

In Germany, Minister of Defense Karl-Theodor zu Guttenberg,

a charismatic Bavarian aristocrat who was the country's most popular politician and widely regarded a future chancellor, was forced to withdraw from politics. Why? Because online activists demanded that that he pay for his sin—which was, years earlier, to have plagiarized some three-fourths of his four-hundred-page doctoral thesis. Zu Guttenberg fought to keep his job. Chancellor Angela Merkel mounted a vigorous defense on his behalf. And just before he finally agreed to resign (in 2011), an overwhelming majority of Germans surveyed (73 percent) strongly preferred that he remain in office. Still, the Internet activists—who insisted that zu Guttenberg be treated the same as everyone else—ultimately prevailed. The online campaign against him was so relentless that he finally felt he had no choice but to withdraw from public life, at least for a time.

Americans who do not have power, authority, and influence are by now practiced at using the Internet to defy, or at least circumvent, those who do. One example involves the impact of the wired world on the written word. First, increasing numbers of writers are simply bypassing potential publishers. Since writers can now deliver their work to their readers directly, electronically, why give publishers a cut, or depend on them for editing and marketing, or bestow on them certain rights, as it were, such as the right to deny or delay publication? Second, a growing numbers of professors, professionals, experts of all sorts, sick and tired of the grueling, often demeaning, rite of subjecting themselves to peer review in order to be published in prestigious journals, have taken to bypassing the process entirely. They present their research directly, online, thereby reaching a far larger audience much more quickly and easily than was possible before. Third, as we all know by now, the power of old media has been seriously weakened, threatened everywhere by online journalism. New media has replaced old media altogether, or reduced it to a semblance of its former self, or at least supplemented it to the point where the many are being given a say while seasoned journalists, their "authority and expertise" of diminished importance, are obliged to share the stage.[32]

Again, sea changes like these can be good or bad, depending on your point of view. In any case, the online trafficking of voices demanding to make a difference has had a corrosive, coarsening effect, the anonymity of such voices allowing anyone and everyone to get away with much more than they would otherwise. "Why," asks literary editor Leon Wieseltier, "does technology exonerate the kind of foul expression that you would not tolerate anywhere else?"[33]

While American culture has been complicated if not corrupted by technology, which seems so often to incite those at the extremes while muting those in the middle, the wired world is, obviously, a fact of twenty-first-century life. Of its effect on the political establishment John Heilemann wrote, "Adapting to the new age of radical transparency rather than resisting it won't be easy. . . . But what Assange and [Facebook cofounder and CEO Mark] Zuckerberg have taught us is that this new age, predicted since the dawn of the web, is upon us."[34] And of its effect on the corporate establishment, Ori Brafman and Rod Beckstrom wrote, "The implications of the Internet for decentralization are profound. . . . The Internet not only makes it easier for people to communicate but provides fertile ground for a host of new decentralized organizations."[35]

Using information technology to overthrow the old is, as we have seen, not new. Martin Luther employed a newfangled device, the printing press, to foment revolt against the authority of the papacy. In late-eighteenth-century America it was newspapers that did this sort of work, convincing "colonial readers of their personal stake in political protests against the English crown." And in mid- to late-twentieth-century Europe, specifically in the Soviet bloc, dissidents used copy and fax machines to incite against communist autocrats in the Soviet Union and East Europe. So the Internet is only the latest iteration of technologies that have for centuries been used by the many without power, authority, and influence against the few with. Of course this does presuppose that the gatekeepers— those in control of the Internet—keep the gates open.

In his book *The Future of Power*, Joseph S. Nye Jr. looks at cyber-power from a global perspective. "World politics will not be the sole province of governments," he writes. Other individuals and institutions are now empowered "to play direct roles in world politics," enabled by the spread of information, by the distribution of power, and by informal networks that "will undercut the monopoly of traditional bureaucracy." Nye concludes that it makes scant sense to ask who dominates in cyberspace, because the barriers to entry in the cyber-domain "are so low that nonstate actors and small states can play significant roles at low levels of cost."[36]

None of this is to suggest that leaders have no arrows left in their quivers. In fact, as just suggested, the independence of the Internet, what is called net neutrality, depends on those with power, authority, and influence, as opposed to those without. Still, resources previously hoarded by those in charge are being dispersed—which is why, as the context has changed, so has leadership, and so has followership.

The implications of all this for the leadership industry—in particular the changes in *context*, in prevailing (democratizing) ideas and in culture and technology; as well as the changes in *followership*, in what people without power, authority, or influence think and feel and do—seem clear to me. In my view, to the degree the industry remains focused, laser-like, on the leader it is doing a disservice to itself and to those who pay good money to learn how to lead. Even the nomenclature, or at least the implications thereof, seem increasingly outdated. At a moment in history when the leader is so obviously weakened, or tarnished, or in some other way relatively disabled; and when what happens in the world at large is so obviously consequential; and when so many followers are not in the least inclined actually to follow, the traditional view of "the leader," the suggestion that "the leader" is all-important, is simply passé.

Part II

Shifting Sands

4

Social Contract—*undermining the understanding*

Evolutionary leadership theory argues that since humans live in groups, and since groups with leaders do better than groups without, leadership and followership were as critical to the survival of ancestral humans as they are to their contemporary counterparts.[1] Certainly since time immemorial there has been between leaders and followers a *social contract*—in which the leader, whether despot or democrat, is generally expected to control the action, while followers are generally expected to go along. Sometimes, of course, this contract gets violated. Still, for all practical purposes, these have been the assumptions on which collective life has been organized—in groups and communities, in institutions and organizations, and at the level of the nation-state.

But as we have seen, leadership has changed and so has followership. The assumptions on which the contract is based are being challenged on a regular basis, not by the few but by the many, and generally in ways that are technologically revolutionary. The nature of the challenge varies, of course. At the one extreme is the expansion of political democracy—ordinary people expecting now to be heard and to participate in collective decision making. At the other extreme is the hostile takeover—challenges to power and authority somewhere along the spectrum from covert resistance to outright rebellion. The result in any case is uncertainty—uncertainty as to whether the contract between leaders and followers still holds and, if it does, what exactly it looks like.

In times past, the contract between leaders and followers was based on traditional sources of power and authority. They included, for example, *might*, as in might makes right; and *heredity*, which entitled the son of a king one day himself to be king; and *charisma*, which depended on the leader's personal capacity to attract, even enthrall, groups of followers. More recently, the contract evolved into something more equitable. Might no longer makes right, certainly not in theory and certainly not in countries or companies considered exemplars of good governance. Nepotism, while hardly obsolete, is a much less legitimate claim to power and authority than it used to be. And in this day and age, again for reasons of culture and technology, charisma is difficult to sustain.[2] Moreover, for their part, ordinary people—followers—have at least since the Enlightenment increasingly insisted on a measure of equity, a trend that in the last half century has only accelerated.

So the assumptions on which the contract is based have changed, first, because the old justifications for having power, authority, and influence are no longer so persuasive, and second, because people in the present think of themselves as more important, more entitled, than did people in the past. What, then, is the basis of the contract in the second decade of the twenty-first century? What reasons do followers now have for going along with leaders? There are only two: either we go along because we *have* to (or think we do), or we go along because we *want to*. In general, the first applies to the workplace. Subordinates go along with their superiors because they think they must to avoid the risk of losing their jobs. And in general, the second applies to the community at large. Good governance, including good corporate governance, implies that the contract between leaders (governors) and followers (governed) is based on *merit*: merit is the basis of the exchange between the presumably estimable leader on the one hand, and the presumably pliable follower on the other.

In theory, at least, we presume that people get elected president or prime minister, or for that matter mayor, because they *deserve* to, because their capacities attest to the legitimacy of their claims to power, authority, and influence. And, similarly, we presume that people are selected to be chief executive officer based on their *excellence*, a professional history that testifies to their superiority as leaders and managers. Further, we believe that political leaders hold to their end of the bargain when government is functional—when it protects against threats foreign and domestic. And we believe that corporate leaders hold to their end of the bargain when business is functional—when it makes money and provides jobs.

This, then, has been the arrangement for at least the last one hundred years. Among other reasons, as governments grew in size, and as corporations became organizations, arranging the collective in accordance with merit simply made good sense. More work needed to be done and more people were required to do it. So it was obvious that the best way to arrange the group was hierarchically, and the best people to slot at the top were those who were both honest and competent. In short, for a century or more, democratic leadership particularly has been, or was presumed by the majority to be, a *meritocracy*, which is why we came to conclude that anyone can be a leader—so long as he or she has the right stuff.

So what exactly is "the right stuff"? What, more precisely, does meritorious leadership consist of? The answer is deceptively simple, for no matter how gussied up the language, no matter how many leadership traits, skills, characteristics, and capacities you can think to name, leadership is judged on only two criteria: *ethics* and *effectiveness*. A good leader is presumed to be ethical. And a good leader is presumed to be effective. Conversely, a bad leader is unethical, ineffective, or both. It's as simple as that—which is precisely the problem.

For as the culture has changed and technology along with it, followers are familiar with the flaws of leaders, with the foibles of leaders, as they never were before. What this familiarity has bred is contempt. Put directly, when the contract between leaders and followers is based on merit, as opposed to self-interest, the game changes. That is, if merit is perceived to be lacking, either because the leader is seen as being in some serious way corrupt, or because the leader is seen as being in some serious way inept, the contract is weakened or even abrogated altogether. Again, we go along with our leaders and managers, particularly in the workplace, for any number of self-interested reasons, including the benefits of material reward and the fear of personal or professional punishment. But the best reason, certainly the ideal reason, to follow, is that we *want* to follow—because we genuinely believe in the integrity and competence of those with power, authority, and influence. Small wonder, then, that when merit matters most, and when merit is viewed as meager or even absent altogether, disappointment and disillusionment set in.

This, in a nutshell, explains why political America has come to be considered nearly ungovernable, and why corporate America is viewed as little short of rapacious. Since so many leaders seem to so many followers to be inept or corrupt, hapless or greedy, Americans have changed, gradually but ineffably, into a nation of malcontents: unwilling to support those in charge unless they must, and unable ourselves to fix what's broken. Add to this disappointment the fact that many followers increasingly feel entitled and act emboldened, and you have a difficult mix, one spelling trouble for individuals and institutions not only in the United States but, as we know by now, the world over.

The Roman Catholic Church—which was obliged in the last ten years to disclose information previously kept secret—presents a striking case in point. Once this private material became public knowledge, the church was revealed as never before and the response was, similarly, as never before. As the story unfolds, note the shift in power and influence away from the traditional church hierarchy, with the pope at the top, to those who in this particular realm heretofore had little or no power or influence: lay Catholics, ordinary priests, the press and the public, courts of law, and the thousands who themselves were abused, but who had stayed silent for so long, right into the twenty-first century.

Undermining the Understanding—in the Catholic Church

In the last decade, the Catholic Church endured a crisis of confidence. To have witnessed church officials, from the pope on down, succumb to the demands of the people has been to witness the diminution of institutional power, the devaluation of positional authority, and the decline of personal influence.

At the heart of what happened is information—information about priestly abuse that became public knowledge only recently. Here then is the key question: why was this information revealed only now, in first decade of the twenty-first century? By now we know that such abuse had been a fact of Catholic life for decades or longer, and that within the church itself this abuse was as well known as it was covered up. So what is it about this moment in time that has made it so conducive to church followers taking on church leaders?

As we have seen, sagas like these are not signaled by the strike of a gong. While in the United States cases of priestly abuse occasionally surfaced beginning in the 1980s, the first big story on this highly charged subject did not break until November 1992. It was a headline in the *Boston Globe* that read "Breaking the Silence: The Church and Sexual Abuse."[3] The article was about five hundred priests who were meeting in a seminary in Massachusetts to address a spate of notorious abuse cases, mainly involving one Father James Porter, a former priest from Fall River. It was charged that between 1960 and 1972, Porter had molested some two hundred minors, a number of whom had recently come forward to claim "violent rape, cruel humiliation, and punishment that can only be described as sadistic."

Notwithstanding this striking, even shattering headline, during the subsequent decade the larger truth remained hidden. While with the benefit of hindsight we can see the gathering storm, at the time the problem seemed minor, a rare rotten apple in the barrel. (The sequence of events foreshadowed, nearly exactly, the sex abuse scandal at Penn State, which broke a decade later.)

January 2002 was the tipping point. Another *Globe* headline— this one read "Church Allowed Abuse by Priest for Years"—changed the church once and for all. The article described how more than 130 persons had recently come forward with "horrific childhood tales," again involving a former priest, this time John J. Geoghan, who had allegedly "fondled or raped" them over a thirty-year period. During the ensuing months the long history of Geoghan's transgressions became as obvious as it was egregious, and the evidence of a long-standing cover-up in the Archdiocese of Boston was damning.

Cardinal Bernard Law had been supreme clerical authority in the Boston area for some eighteen years. His initial response to the crisis was chilly and distant. It was insufficient to the nature and magnitude of the crimes—and, it turned out, to the temper of the times. This initial failure, this apparent lack of adequate compassion and contrition, explains why followers, lay Catholics especially, started, at first slowly, then more quickly and decisively, to take matters into their own hands. Ordinary people morphed into Participants and Activists who in the ensuing months protested against Law in particular and against the archdiocese more generally. As winter became spring it was apparent that Law, at least, was in trouble. Among the resisters was a group calling itself Voice of the Faithful—which was so dedicated, well organized, and skilled at mobilizing civilized resistance to the existing ecclesiastical power structure that, more than any other single element of the protest movement, it turned the tide.

Law had wavered between denying and demurring, and accepting and apologizing. But during late summer and fall of 2002, the battle lines hardened between the increasingly ineffectual cardinal on the one side and the increasingly fierce resisters on the other. Law's critics felt freer than before to ridicule his responses to the dreadful disclosures; he, meanwhile, turned inward, hunkered down. By November it was clear the crisis was coming to its inexorable end: the Activists would not let up, and for all his power, authority, and influence, the cardinal had met his match.

The straw that broke the cardinal's back was, not surprisingly, information—the release of more than two thousand pages of previously secret documents providing further evidence that the archdiocese's feckless, reckless handling of notoriously abusive priests was not an aberration, but rather standard operating procedure. On December 10 it was reported that fifty-eight priests from the Boston area had signed a letter to Law urging him to quit his post. On December 12 it was reported that Law and at least five other bishops had received subpoenas to appear before a grand jury. And on December 13 it was reported that Pope John Paul II, "in a dramatic recognition of the damage done to the church by Law's repeated failure to remove abusive priests from the ministry," had accepted the cardinal's resignation.

So ended a seismic series of events in modern church history—lay Catholics had forced out a highly placed church official and an ugly truth was revealed. It was revealed that in order to protect its reputation, the church, and certainly the Boston Archdiocese, had for decades concealed crimes against minors.

Again, why exactly did this story, this information, come to light only in the first decade of the twenty-first century? Because by then the context within which the story was situated had changed—by then the faithful were no longer willing to be passive, the media were no longer afraid to step on toes heretofore sacrosanct, judges were no longer timid about ordering access to files long since sealed, and because by then the social contract, in this case between the church hierarchy and lay Catholics, was no longer considered ironclad.

Nor did the story—which turned out highly contagious—end in Boston. Not by a long shot. A 2004 report enumerated some eleven thousand abuse allegations, covering 95 percent of Catholic dioceses in the United States. Moreover, in the years since, the scandal has swept through Germany, Belgium, and the Netherlands, with highly publicized cases in other countries in Europe and elsewhere, including Britain, Italy, France, Malta, Switzerland, Austria, Mexico, New Zealand, Canada, Kenya, the Philippines, and Australia.

Meanwhile, Pope John Paul II's successor, Benedict XVI, in part because of the situation he faced when he took office in 2005, and in part because of his own lackluster reaction to the situation, was weakened by the crisis. He was weakened with regard to the authority of his position, and with regard to the power and influence of his particular persona. To begin his record more generally was mixed. As Russell Shorto has pointed out, Benedict's papacy had already been beleaguered by controversy—each example of which, again unprecedented in modern history, raised objections to his leadership. Add to this his initially tepid response to disclosures of priestly abuse and you had a widespread impression of a pope who, besides being tough and conservative, was insensitive and out of touch.[4]

By 2010 the pope seemed finally to acknowledge the seriousness of the situation: In March of that year he wrote a letter to Irish Catholics that said he was "truly sorry" for Ireland's history of priestly abuse. In April 2010 the Vatican issued an "introductory guide" to explain church rules on reporting abuse. In May 2010, in a "marked shift in tone," the pope admitted the problem lay not with victims or with the media, but with "sin inside the church."[5] In June 2010 he asked for forgiveness from God and from victims of sexual abuse and pledged the church would do "everything possible" to prevent future abuse. In July 2010 the Vatican announced it had tightened rules for disciplining cases of sexual abuse, marking the first time church law had been changed in response to the scandal. Finally, in December 2010, Pope Benedict XVI acknowledged the sexual abuse scandal had reached "a degree we could not have imagined." In a pointed message to the Vatican hierarchy, he added, "We must ask ourselves what was wrong in our proclamation, in our whole way of living the Christian life, to allow such a thing to happen."

Notwithstanding the pope's efforts to restore to his papacy the legitimacy it had enjoyed under his predecessor, John Paul II, his battle is likely a losing one. For it turns out that religious leaders are not exempt from the same twenty-first-century forces aligned against political and business leaders. Consider the following. First, cables obtained in December 2010 by WikiLeaks confirm continuing challenges to Vatican officials by local bishops and civil authorities. Second, technology continues to undermine the authority of the church, just as it undermines authority everywhere else. For example, in Ireland, where the abuse crisis was particularly horrific and, as a result, had major consequences (Prime Minister Enda Kenny rebuked "the dysfunction, the disconnection, the elitism" that "dominate the culture of the Vatican"), a website was set up, "CountMeOut," to walk thousands of Catholics through the process of defecting from the church. Third, the scandal continues to spread: in 2011 it was revealed that the Archdiocese of Philadelphia had provided safe haven to thirty-seven priests accused of behaving inappropriately or abusively toward minors, and that most remained still active in the ministry. And a Kansas City bishop was indicted for failure to report a case of suspected child abuse—the first time the leader of an American diocese was held criminally liable for the behavior of a priest he supervised. Fourth, the scandal is costly, literally: in December 2010, $30 million was awarded in compensatory damages to an American man who said he was sexually abused by a priest more than one hundred times. Fifth, explanations for what happened still seem to many to be lame—such as the "blame Woodstock" excuse, which came out of a five-year study commissioned by America's Roman Catholic bishops. The study, released in 2011, essentially said that the abuse had occurred because poorly prepared priests were affected by the social and political turmoil of the 1960s and '70s.

And, finally, it seems nearly certain that the pope would not of his own accord have responded to the scandal as he did, in repeatedly expressing contrition. Rather he did so because he was pressured to do so—by some inside the church and by some without. As reported by the *New York Times*, the "Vatican took action only after bishops from English-speaking nations become so concerned about resistance from top church officials" that a secret meeting was held to hear their complaints. Change was, in other words, the result of political pressure from, among others, "prelates from across the globe collectively pressing their superiors for reform."[6]

These prelates testify to the fact that patterns of dominance and deference have changed inside the church, just as they have changed nearly everywhere else. In 2011 there was further evidence when Benedict presided over the beatification of John Paul II. Normally such a ceremony is absent conflict—but not this time. This time questions were raised far and wide not only about the uncommon alacrity with which John Paul was being beatified, but also about whether his beatification was even justified. Given that John Paul had been among the many in the church hierarchy who had ignored, downplayed, or concealed abuse, his first step on the journey to sainthood was polarizing because it raised yet again the question of merit. From everything we know now about John Paul, the question was whether he was indeed a church leader who, on account of his unimpeachable ethics and extraordinary efficacy, deserved to be sanctified.

Undermining the Understanding— in American Politics

In politics as in religion, the contract between leaders and followers looks something like this: I, the follower, will do what you, the leader, want me to do so long as you keep to our agreement—so long as you are reasonably honest and reasonably competent. But if you are not, the contract between us frays. Under such a circumstance

I owe you little or even no allegiance, and I am entitled to withhold my support.

There are further similarities: for example, in politics as in religion, we expect our leaders minimally to mirror our ideological or spiritual preferences. (In business, such similar sentiments are less important.) But the issue that concerns us here is information: what happens to the contract between political leaders and ordinary Americans when what the latter learn about the former throws into question their ethics and efficacy? We have seen what happened in the Catholic Church when followers lost the faith not in their religion but in their religious leaders—there was resistance. Similarly we will see later on how the American people resist en masse—by circumventing the existing system and starting a social or political movement. How, though, do they resist on an individual level? What do they do, or not do, to show their displeasure with leaders who disappoint?

To answer these questions, I do as I have done all along: I divide the whole into three *equal* parts: the *leader,* the *followers,* and the *context* within which they are embedded. Only by taking into account all three simultaneously can we come to understand how the American people resist their political leaders, from the president on down.

To begin, we look at the president's persona: never before have our chief executives been as personally and professionally vulnerable as they are now. We scrutinize their every move, analyze and criticize not only what they do in the present, but what they did in the past. So, Barack Obama, for example, has been looked at every which way: where he was born; what was the impact on him of his black African father and his white American mother; what is the nature of his faith and of his marriage; how does his mind work and what motivates him; what is his core character and is he introverted or extroverted; what is the nature of his leadership style; and what, given everything we know about him, will he do next?

This brings us to the leader's position. Whether president or prime minister, chancellor or royal, senator or mayor, the office at the top has been diminished—and is unlikely ever to be restored to its former glory. The trappings are still there, of course: the White House, the Kremlin, 10 Downing Street, Élysée Palace. But the power of these places as symbols no longer translates into authority—to which the office of president of the United States attests.

George C. Edwards III has written about the limits of presidential power in the twenty-first century. He concludes that no matter who is in the Oval Office, followers of every sort are little inclined to, well, follow. *All* recent presidents have had a difficult time leading the public. "Relying on going public to pressure Congress when the public is unlikely to be responsive to the president's appeals is a recipe for failure." And *all* recent presidents have had a difficult time leading the Congress. "There is not a single systematic study that demonstrates that presidents can reliably move members of Congress, especially members of the opposition party, to support them." In short, "Barack Obama is only the latest in a long line of presidents who have not been able to transform the political landscape through their efforts of persuasion"—who have not been able to exert influence.[7] No matter the president's persona, or even the situational specifics, his followers, whether the political elite or the public at large, are more disposed to resist him than to support him. This syndrome was especially evident during the 2011 budget-ceiling talks, which were nothing less than a fiasco. No one was *able* to lead, certainly not the nation's chief executive—and no one was *willing* to follow.

It turns out, then, that times are difficult not only for dictatorial leaders but for democratic leaders as well. Our familiarity with and disrespect for our leaders, coupled with our feeling entitled and being emboldened, saps their authority, which then drains their power and influence.

Still, for the last few decades, though the level of political resistance in America has been high, it has generally tended, at least on an individual level, to be muted. To the dismay of observers such as philosopher and activist Cornel West, who wait impatiently for plain people to prepare themselves for "life and death confrontations with the powers that be," many Americans are Isolates—they opt out of politics altogether.[8] Many others are Bystanders—they stand and watch but do not in any way participate. Participants, in turn, sometimes support the opposition, occasionally engaging in protests, more often by taking out their angers and frustrations online, bitching and moaning anonymously, from one electoral cycle to the next. Of course Americans do also vote—though not in large numbers. Only about half of eligible American voters bother to cast a ballot, even for president. (For other elected officials, the percentage of voters is far lower.) And they do also participate in polls—in those seemingly ubiquitous surveys, which simply mirror the grim national mood. In August 2011, Gallup pollsters posed this question: "In general, are you satisfied with the way things are going in the United States at this time?" Only a miserable 11 percent of those polled answered in the affirmative. (Gallup began measuring national satisfaction in 1979. The numbers in summer 2011 were among the lowest ever recorded.)

Finally, of course, there are some numbers of Activists who register their resistance loudly, clearly, and consistently the old-fashioned way, that is, in the streets. In 2011 tens of thousands publicly protested for weeks or even months on end against union-busting bills in states including Wisconsin, Ohio, and Indiana. In Wisconsin, where angry voters were strongly motivated and well organized, they did more: they prevented Republican governor Scott Walker's candidate from scoring an easy electoral victory in a race for state supreme court justice, and they mounted a recall effort against the governor himself. But of course the most glaring example of public protest in recent years, of old-fashioned political activism, is Occupy Wall Street, which turned out larger and more disruptive than originally anticipated. As we will see in the next chapter, online efforts to change the world can be extremely effective. But they do not and cannot replace entirely the passion of numbers of political activists assembled in one place, marching together for whatever their cause.

So many weakened leaders, so many alienated followers, and such an array of apparently intractable problems—this constitutes the cantankerous context within which political leadership in twenty-first-century America is expected to be exercised. No wonder it's so hard. For even though democracy is preferred nearly everywhere, preferred to other sorts of arrangements between leaders and followers, democratic leadership, especially in a system as structurally fractured as that of the United States—federal, state, and local; executive, legislative, and judicial—does not seem to provide good answers to hard problems, at least not now. Of course when times are tough—when unemployment is high and the city of Shanghai has a significantly lower rate of infant mortality than does the city of New York—the systemic difficulties to which I allude are exacerbated.

These are not, I might add, issues the leadership industry is particularly prepared or poised to address. Given its fixation on the leader, its dismissal of the follower, and its avoidance of the larger context within which leaders and followers the world over necessarily are embedded, the industry is not by and large ready, willing, or even able to take on the most vexing of our collective concerns.

To be sure, the picture I paint should not be seen as unremittingly grim. There are times when followers in the political arena, just like followers in other arenas, support their leaders—eagerly, enthusiastically, and without reservation. This does not, however, fundamentally alter the twenty-first-century template: followers less likely than before to assess their leaders as honest and competent, and therefore more likely than before to feel alienated and act angry. Though this chronic condition is widely interpreted as reflecting political differences, it is better understood as reflecting the temper of the times, in which followers are dissatisfied to the point of being disillusioned.

Undermining the Understanding—in American Business

Like the contract between leaders and followers in American politics, the contract between leaders and followers in American business has been undermined for one good and simple reason: because of the information to which followers now have access, too many leaders are judged by too many followers to be unethical or incompetent or both.

Why bestow on you my loyalty when you do not merit it? Why follow where you lead when you are not worthy of my fealty? Again, we usually do follow when to follow is in our interest—particularly when our livelihoods are at stake. But, as the polls attest, we do not do so gladly: the majority of Americans have tuned out or been turned off. They, we, are dismayed by our leaders, corporate as well as political, distressed by what seems their chronic inability to get the United States "moving again," while other countries, some only recently labeled "developing," overtake us by nearly every significant measure.

So what has been our response? It has not been to abrogate the contract entirely—hardly. In fact, notwithstanding increased income inequity and increased unemployment, Americans in recent years have not, at least in any significant numbers, joined unions, forced out bad leaders, punished them for performing poorly, or even, until recently, taken to the streets. Nor, notwithstanding some exceptions, do Americans opt out—they do not quit the institutions and organizations of which they are members, or leave the United States for greener pastures elsewhere. Rather they register their displeasures in other ways—by taking the path of least resistance. On an individual level at least, they resist quietly rather than noisily, so as not to risk either their tenure in the workplace or their entrenchment in the community.

In corporate America, what does such low-level resistance look like? How do corporate subordinates resist their corporate superiors? And how do others—shareholders, say, and pundits, and ordinary people—respond to America's corporate elite? They take one of three different tacks: they go on the attack, they turn to the law, or they besmirch the reputations of those more powerful than they.

Attacks on leaders by followers run the gamut. Some are as relatively harmless as leveling the playing field. For instance, the website Glassdoor.com is a new arrow in the quiver of employees to use against employers. Described as a "free career community where anyone can find and anonymously share an inside look at jobs and companies," Glassdoor.com has information on more than a million workplace salaries, company reviews, and other materials intended to help ordinary people manage their careers—and their leaders and managers.

Other sorts of attacks by the weak against the strong are more serious, such as those by shareholder activists. For a constellation of reasons that I, at least, bemoan—for example, the time, money, and research it takes to monitor such things as executive compensation—shareholder activism has failed so far to be a major force for major change. This is not, however, to say that shareholder activists are enfeebled altogether.[9] Executive pay, for example, is more tightly aligned with performance than it was twenty years ago.[10] Royal Dutch Shell is a case in point: in 2009 shareholders dealt management a blow by shooting down its executive compensation plan. And there are other signs of life, especially in Europe and the United States.[11] In the United States there has been a sharp rise in shareholder activism, particularly to encourage socially responsible investing. According to *Proxy Preview 2011*, "nearly 400 environmental and social shareholder resolutions were filed in the latest proxy season for issues ranging from labor and human rights to supply chain impacts and recycling."[12] In fact, in the energy sector alone, the number of shareholder resolutions soared some 50 percent during the 2011 proxy season.

Along similar lines, companies such as General Electric and Walt Disney have responded to shareholder criticisms by agreeing to change, if only slightly, their compensation practices. GE announced it would put new conditions on two million stock options it had granted CEO Jeffrey Immelt only a year before—a move that, according to the *Wall Street Journal*, underscored not only the "pressure on Mr. Immelt to get the company growing again" but also "shareholders' increasing clout regarding matters of executive compensation."[13] And just days before a potential "no" vote on CEO Robert Iger's pay package, Disney dropped its plan to pay Iger and three other executives extra "excise" taxes on money made if they were forced to leave—a move that in turn led shareholder watchdog groups to change their say-on-pay recommendation from a "no" vote to a "yes."[14]

Finally, shareholder activists are starting, even if only slowly, to use social media. Up until now, individual and institutional investors have only occasionally employed sites such as Twitter and Facebook to muster support for a cause—likely because social media are not second nature to investors, who, among other things, tend to be older rather than younger. Still, indications are that restiveness in business will begin to resemble restiveness in politics; that is, it will eventually find an outlet on the Internet.

Activist investors are already using online technologies, for example, to connect and rally with other shareholders, participate in annual meetings, coordinate proxy votes, and complain loudly if not particularly effectively about company policies including executive compensation. Some of Wall Street's most prominent players are paying attention, including David Rubenstein, cofounder of the private equity giant Carlyle Group. In 2011 Rubenstein made something of a prediction: "Let's suppose somebody wants to buy a company and has to get shareholder approval," he said. "Employees and shareholders could use Facebook to rally support against an acquisition."[5]

Such an appeal would not be unprecedented. In 2007 a private investor by the name of Eric Jackson went online to detail—and denigrate—Yahoo's management strategy. First he won over small shareholders, and then he went on to large institutions, enabling him ultimately to play a significant role in the fall of Yahoo's chief executive, Terry Semel. Clearly, in order for individual shareholder activists such as Jackson to create change, they need the support of a critical mass, of enough investors similarly exercised. But, under the right circumstances, shareholders can change quickly from being Isolates and Bystanders to being Participants and even Activists. In fact, a number of online sites make it their business to facilitate just this sort of transition. One, Moxy Vote, which is billed as a "proxy adviser for the individual," has thousands of users, and claims at least one major success. In order to block an initial take-over bid on On2 Technologies by Google, it rallied the target's small shareholders. Eventually Google sweetened its offer by 25 percent.[16]

Given the lack of obvious ways for the corporate weak to take on the corporate strong, especially given the decline in union membership and the lack of significant public protest, at least until 2011, aggrieved individuals and groups have turned to the courts to right what's wrong. For various reasons—money being the most obvious—legal recourse is hardly an everyday occurrence. But when the law does intervene on the side of followers, the consequences can be significant. Workers against Wal-Mart is a prime example—the former charged the latter with having failed to provide employees with everything from proper rest and meal breaks to proper compensation. Ultimately, to dispose of sixty-three different suits, Wal-Mart in 2008 agreed to settle, to the tune of $640 million. The company further consented to electronically document its compliance with labor laws, having clearly concluded that bad publicity was bad for business. Said Wal-Mart's general counsel in a prepared statement, "Resolving this litigation is in the best interest of our company, our shareholders, and our associates."[17]

Nor was this the only case in which Wal-Mart was sued by employees convinced they were treated unfairly. In fact, Wal-Mart was at the receiving end of the largest civil rights class-action suit in U.S. history, potentially exposing it to billions of dollars in damages. In the federal gender discrimination case of *Dukes v. Wal-Mart Stores, Inc.*, the company was accused of discriminating against women in promotions, pay, and job assignments, in violation of the 1964 Civil Rights Act. The case was brought by Betty Dukes, who in 2000 alleged that despite her six years of hard work and excellent performance, Wal-Mart had denied her the training she needed to advance to a higher position. Though the Supreme Court ultimately decided for Wal-Mart and against Dukes, the story is far from over. Dukes has gone on record as saying, "We are still determined to move forward and to present our case in court," and lawyers for the plaintiffs have vowed to press ahead.[18] Meanwhile, in part at least to forestall and foreclose legal liability at some later point, Wal-Mart went ahead and instituted some changes. In 2011 it announced significant new programs aimed at helping women-owned businesses and women workers, projecting its investment in these programs to be fully $20 billion.

Additionally, the law is used by governments (federal and state), acting on behalf of ordinary people, to preclude future business leaders from repeating the transgressions of past business leaders. For example, the 2002 Sarbanes-Oxley Act—a response to corporate scandals involving companies such as Enron, WorldCom, and Tyco—was passed in an attempt to set more stringent standards for corporate governance and financial practice. While Sarbanes-Oxley did not, obviously, forestall the financial crisis of just a few years later, it was precursor to another, somewhat similar, bill, the 2010 Dodd-Frank Wall Street Reform and Consumer Protection Act. Predictably, many of the best and brightest have since derided this bill, as they did the one previous, as inadequate to the task. Dodd-Frank will not, they say, stop banks from being too big to fail; or preclude new financial vehicles intended only to make money; or intrude on greed as a major motivator. As Wall Street watcher William Cohan puts it, "We're no better protected from bankers' potentially reckless behavior than we were before the latest round of reforms."[19] Still, Dodd-Frank does do something, such as providing new protections for consumers, specifically through the U.S. Consumer Financial Protection Bureau, and promoting transparency.

The law is used to protect the weak against the strong in other ways as well. The European Commission has suggested mandatory prison terms for crimes such as insider trading, and in the United States individuals and institutions are, occasionally at least, prosecuted, convicted, and sentenced for corporate wrongdoing. More than two years after Lehman Brothers imploded, the attorney general of the state of New York sued the accounting firm Ernst & Young for engaging in a "massive accounting fraud" by misleading investigators about the investment bank's financial health. A California lawsuit is seeking class-action status, the better to charge Apple, Google, Intel, and other tech companies of violating antitrust laws by conspiring to fix employee pay and limiting their opportunities by agreeing to "no solicitation" deals, which preclude companies from hiring employees away from each other.[20] A couple of political activists, Nancy and Derek Casady, are suing American International Group (AIG), Goldman Sachs, and Deutsche Bank, charging they engaged in fraudulent and speculative transactions incurring billions of dollars of losses. And former top executives now serving long sentences in prison include Dennis Kozlowski (Tyco International), Jeffrey Skilling (Enron), Bernard Ebbers (WorldCom), Lee Farkas (Taylor, Bean & Whitaker), and Raj Rajaratnam (Galleon Group).

Finally, followers diminish or even destroy reputations. There is that old saying, "Sticks and stones will hurt my bones, but names will never hurt me." But that's not quite true. The relentless attacks on individuals and institutions in the corporate sector do carry a cost, though in many cases it is nonfinancial and difficult to calculate. Still, the attacks are personal and professional, they appear in old media and new, and they are leveled both by experts and ordinary people—by whoever is fed up to here with those in charge. Put briefly, instead of staging revolutions, we damage reputations.

Even the Oracle of Omaha, the generally irreproachable, unimpeachable Warren Buffett, ended up grist for this mill. After it seemed he was snookered and suckered by top associate David Sokol,

Buffett became an object of scorn, nearly overnight. Of course, he had asked for it, in a way, having years ago declared he would sooner lose money than even a shred of his reputation. Buffett was not, in any case, spared. His lack of response to the Sokol debacle was variously described by experts and pundits as inexplicable, reprehensible, or hypocritical. Things got so bad that Buffett finally felt compelled to backtrack. After being criticized sharply by his shareholders at the 2011 meeting of Berkshire Hathaway—normally such gatherings are lovefests—Buffett assured the assembled, his faithful, nearly worshipful followers, that Berkshire would "try to minimize mistakes we make in the future." Additionally, in response to the public pressure, he changed his tune. Having earlier insisted that he did not consider Sokol's actions to be "in any way unlawful," Buffett now described them as "inexcusable" and admitted that there was some "very damaging evidence" against his former associate.

Exiting the Understanding

If you are dissatisfied with a contract to which you are a party, and if you want unilaterally to change it, you can upend it, or circumvent it. Entrepreneurs choose the second over the first: neither leaders nor followers, they opt out, taking it on themselves to try something new and different.

Entrepreneurship—as in "social entrepreneurship" or "entrepreneurial leadership"—has never been more popular, more attractive to young people in particular than it is now. In fact, whereas it used to be all about "becoming a leader," today becoming an entrepreneur, or an "entrepreneurial leader" who is visionary as well as transformational, is equally in fashion. Schools of business especially are accommodating this newfound passion, having added in the last few years countless programs, courses, and other sorts of learning experiences specifically targeted at those who would be entrepreneurs.

The entrepreneur—someone with a vision of a venture of some sort, who proceeds then somehow to launch it—has been around for centuries. Why, then, has entrepreneurship become only recently so attractive an alternative? One reason is that the entrepreneur operates outside the traditional organizational hierarchy at a time when the traditional organizational hierarchy is no longer so appealing. Entrepreneurship implies the absence of leaders and managers as conventionally understood—as well as the absence of followers. Instead entrepreneurship connotes something more freewheeling and swashbuckling, creative and atypical as opposed to conventional and predictable. Put in terms that I have used here, the entrepreneur refuses to sign the standard contract between leaders and followers. He or she exists outside it, neither the one party nor the other, nor beholden in an obvious way to an arrangement between those more dominant and those more deferent.

Another reason entrepreneurship is now so attractive an alternative is that it has become obvious that neither government nor business, nor even any other existing institution (such as nonprofits), is able comprehensively to address what ails us. So entrepreneurs step in—they fill a need.

Entrepreneurs, whether social or corporate, can be divided into two broad categories: they are individuals, or they are groups—-people acting in concert to address a problem that no one else has been willing or able fully to solve. Examples of social entrepreneurship are especially instructive, because they typically take on situations that others find impossibly daunting.

In the first category—the *individual entrepreneur*—is someone like Elizabeth Scharpf, whose work was described in an article in the

New York Times Magazine: "Why wait for governments or established charities to assist rape victims, orphans or impoverished women when you can start an NGO in your basement and do it yourself?" As the title implies, Scharpf "joined a revolution, so far unnamed because it is just beginning. It's all about what might be called Do-It-Yourself Foreign Aid, because it starts with the proposition that it's not only presidents and United Nations officials who can chip away at global challenges. Passionate individuals with great ideas can do the same, especially in the age of the Internet and social media."[21] Similarly, there is John Prendergast, described as "America's most influential activist in Africa's most troubled regions," who managed almost single-handedly to focus on war-torn Sudan the attention of a range of influential players, from President Obama to actor and activist George Clooney.[22] And there is Ravindra Misal, himself born in India to a low-caste laboring family, now a self-made man determined to be a "caste buster," to eliminate insofar as he is able the old, hidebound system that very nearly trapped him forever. Misal is an example of "the type of person who will truly transform India: not an engineer or a financier, but an average person who refused to be satisfied with the status he was born to."[23] A final example, though he would never call himself either an entrepreneur or a leader, is Javier Sicilia. Sicilia is a poet turned activist, whose Movement for Peace with Justice and Dignity seeks to end drug-related violence in Mexico. In a matter of months the Movement was staging peaceful marches throughout Mexico, inspiring tens of thousands of ordinary people finally to take a stand. One among several reasons Sicilia was able to mobilize Mexicans is because he himself eschews power and authority. As Enrique Krauze put it, "The movement is political, but it exists outside politics."[24]

In the second category, the *entrepreneurial group*, are similarly bold and innovative players including, for example, the following:

the "turtle people," a cluster of ordinary people, environmentalists, who have taken it on themselves to save sea turtles in and around the Gulf of Mexico; members of the Enough Project, started in 2006 by a small group of concerned policy makers and activists determined to build a permanent constituency to prevent genocide and crimes against humanity; a coalition of animal rights groups suing the Ringling Bros. and Barnum & Bailey Circus, charging they manhandle and mistreat their elephants; knots of gay high school students in Utah who convened, in spite of powerful local opposition, the first Gay-Straight Alliance in the history of their conservative, largely Mormon state; and women in the Middle East, such as the Women of the Wall, who are challenging age-old Jewish traditions by publicly praying at the Western Wall alongside men; and others, also women, who are challenging age-old Muslim traditions by attempting in countries such as Saudi Arabia to, for example, drive, vote, and get a job without permission from a male relative. (In response to the push from below, King Abdullah of Saudi Arabia announced in 2011 that for the first time in his country's history, women would be allowed to vote, albeit only in local elections and only in 2015.)

Entrepreneurship is not, incidentally, confined only to those who seem to be tilting at windmills. Going *outside* the system seems sometimes the only way to get anything done—even by those *within* the system. The U.S. Senate's so-called gang of six is an example. The "gang" consisted of three Democratic and three Republican senators who, after despairing of Washington's continuing inability to reduce significantly the national debt, took it on themselves to work for months to draft a viable debt-reduction plan. Of course they never did have a breakthrough—a magic moment in which all hands joined. But the gang of six did model cooperation rather than conflict, they did set the stage for continuing conversation, and they did at least try to address a problem that others had dismissed as unsolvable.

Exiting the understanding or nullifying the social contract in any other way is not, of course, the norm. Leaders—whether popes, presidents, chief executive officers, or lesser lights—are not exactly obsolete. Followers are not necessarily obstructionists. And the contract between them, while weakened, still holds.

What has changed, though, is the logic of the contract. Since twenty-first-century followers follow for only two reasons—either because they have to or because they want to leading is easier for those, such as business and military leaders, in a position to threaten a stick or promise a carrot. The rest must depend on merit, on their being perceived as effective and ethical, a combination of character-istics that at this moment in time seems in lamentably short supply.

This raises again the question of how to learn to lead in the twenty-first century. How to learn to lead when leaders are dimin-ished from what they were, even in the recent past? How to learn to lead when resources such as power, authority, and influence are scarcer than before—and when any number of followers is as likely to be resistant as deferent? And, finally, how to learn to lead when the context itself is fraught with complexity and constraint?

Up to now the assumption has been that, whatever the com-plexities of learning to lead and manage may be, they fall, conve-niently, under the heading of "leadership development." But it is no longer so simple. Now learning about leadership and learning how to lead *must* involve learning about followership and learning how to follow. Moreover, developing *contextual intelligence*, knowledge about and understanding of context, has moved from being of only secondary or even tertiary importance to being of primary impor-tance. It is, in short, a paradigm shift, with crucial implications that must be explored.

5

American Experience—
downgrading leaders

eadership in the United States of America has always been difficult to exercise. Philosophers such as John Locke contributed to the condition, as did the Founders themselves, who used the Revolution to construct a government in which no single individual or institution was likely to dominate for long. Moreover, as historians in our own time have shifted the emphasis from early American leaders to early American followers, that is, to ordinary people, we have come to understand that Americans were resistant to rule from the start. A full two years before the adoption of the Declaration of Independence, the people of the New England countryside had thrown out their royal rulers, declaring themselves ipso facto free and independent of Britain.[1]

What has by now become apparent is that the anti-authority furies that fueled the Revolution left a legacy that was enduring. Equally apparent is that in tandem with America's distant past, America's recent past has strained relations between leaders and followers to the point of dysfunction. As a result, twenty-first-century Americans might be getting the leadership they deserve— but they are not, by and large, getting the leadership they want.

Dysfunctional Body Politic

In a perfect world, we would be blessed with transforming leaders and servant leaders, who live and breathe for the benefit of their followers. In a somewhat less perfect world, we would have leaders who mirrored their followers, who represented them honestly and authentically. Political scientist Jane Mansbridge wrote that in relatively uncorrupt democracies, political life generally produces "intrinsically motivated" leaders, with objectives between voters and their representatives largely aligned, and voters able to easily engage in a reasonable selection process.[2] But in the world in which we actually live, leaders tend to put self-interest ahead of the public interest. In such a circumstance, no one assumes that leaders are morally superior, or that they care fervently about their followers. Rather, we know on some level that leaders and followers are more or less alike—both are plain people, no less and no more beneficent than the rest.

We tend toward optimism: to expect that those we elect, select to attend to the nation's business, will make things better and not worse, will move the nation forward, if only slowly and slightly. But more than before, this hope seems misplaced. In every recent electoral cycle, Americans have soon become disenchanted with their political leaders, disappointed that the land of the free and home of the brave seems at sea. Mired still in a war far from home, recovering still from a recession so severe it will hobble the economy for years to come, oppressed by the national debt, and saddled on a personal level with worries about, among other things, money and work, Americans are suspicious of their political leaders and skeptical they can cure whatever it is that ails us.

The problem in politics is both individual and institutional. American voters, followers, are distrustful of political leaders on an individual level—a fact confirmed in poll after poll, year after year. But they are also distrustful of political leaders on an institutional level. That is, when individual political leaders aggregate in institutions such as the Congress, they are seen as being even less ethical and effective than they are on their own, when they're in their home districts, among their own constituents. Playing well with others is not, in other words, considered their strong suit.

Political experts have for years been lamenting the near breakdown of some of our most venerable institutions, such as, to take one glaring example, the U.S. Senate. Of the chamber that once was the jewel in America's legislative crown, Michael Tomasky writes, "The truth is that no institution of American government is more responsible for our inability to address pressing national problems than the Senate, and no institution is in greater need of reform."[3] George Packer concludes the same, that the Senate is weakened to the point of being broken: it is unable to withstand pressures from outside, particularly those relating to raising money; it is hostile to members with independent minds; it no longer provides any incentive to cooperate across the aisle; and, far from being the "fount of ideas" it used to be, the Senate is instead "a backwater of the U.S. government."[4]

The U.S. Senate is, in short, dysfunctional to the point of national scandal. That senators are, rather like their counterparts in the House of Representatives, unable or unwilling to collaborate to address the most pressing of our national problems testifies to America's leadership crisis. Packer describes scenes that in another day and age would have been shocking: senators giving speeches to virtually empty chambers, not one of their colleagues paying the slightest attention; the presiding officer of the Senate sitting in a chair on the dais, equally inattentive and distracted; quorum calls that amount to time killers; a press gallery once packed, now generally deserted; and an essentially three-day workweek (no Mondays, no Fridays), enabling senators to return home to do what they must to stay in office, which is, of course, to raise money.

The reputation of the Senate has waxed and waned over more than two hundred years of American history. But not so long ago, a senator was still a star, and the Senate itself a prestigious institution that attracted the best and brightest of America's political talent. Packer looks back to those years, the 1960s and '70s, when the "intensity of senatorial purpose" was so strong and the level of institutional performance so high, it "must strike today's legislators as profoundly humbling." Now the context has changed, the culture has changed, and so has the way the Senate works.

The degree of senatorial obstructionism—maneuvering that precludes rather than facilitates legislative action—is at an all-time high. The most obvious example is the filibuster, which was once rare. But now, as Norman Ornstein observes, the threat of filibuster is so common that it actually inverts majority rule, allowing the minority party to block, or at least delay, whatever the legislation it wants to oppose.[5] The constant attempt to block legislation rather than to pass it has led observers to despair of correction. Tomasky concludes that because the prospect of serious change is so remote, we are saddled for the indefinite future with minority rule, leaving the Senate majority paying the political price for gridlock, while problems and crises go unaddressed. Packer thinks that even if somehow filibuster reform were passed, "the Senate will remain a sclerotic, wasteful, unhappy body."

There is a relationship between the decline of the Senate in particular and the decline of political leadership in America more generally. For the Senate was once known as the world's greatest deliberative body. James Madison wrote about the Senate in the *Federalist* papers, making clear he intended for it to have status and stability sufficient to check the popular will—that being the House of Representatives. Madison proposed that members of the Senate, as distinguished from members of the House, be more advanced in age and have a longer period of citizenship. Moreover, once the Constitution was signed, it was decreed that senators serve for six years, longer than any other elected official at the national level.

Thus the decline and dysfunction of the Senate, and indeed of the Congress as a whole, reflect many of the difficulties and debasements that in recent decades are associated with leadership in America: the triumph of self-interest over the public interest; the overweening importance of money in politics; the coarsening of public discourse; the refusal of individuals to collaborate for the common good; the degree to which ideological purity intrudes on political pragmatism; the degree to which the extremes weaken and even govern the center; the degree to which going along to get something done is seen as a weakness; and, finally, our absolute inability, at least so far, to properly fix what's obviously broken.

Members of the Senate have nearly always had some difficulty working with each other, and they have nearly always had some difficulty working with the president. However, while in the past these difficulties were generally overcome to good effect, we live in a time in which collaboration between the executive and legislative branches of government is elusive in the extreme.

Some of this is the consequence of hype. In particular, the constant drumbeat of cable television—channels such as Fox and MSNBC, transfixed by tensions and trivialities and shilling tirelessly for their side—accentuates the negative while nearly eliminating the positive. But it is also true that the American people are more divided now than they were, say, thirty years ago. In 1984, 41 percent of Americans identified themselves as centrists, while 10 percent described themselves as either very liberal or very

conservative. By 2005, the number in the middle dropped to 28 percent, while the number at the two extremes rose to 23 percent.[6] Because these bedeviling divides have grown larger in the last quarter
century, cooperation among political antagonists has become that
much more difficult, if not impossible, to achieve.

The American president is expected to reconcile at least some
of these differences—to bridge the factionalism both among the
American people and among those who represent them. The president is, in other words, expected to lead to unify—at least insofar
as is minimally necessary to tend to the most pressing of the nation's business. But if truth be told, the two most recent presidents,
George W. Bush and Barack Obama, found the task of presidential
leadership in early twenty-first-century America to be daunting. Of
Bush it can be said that after eight years in the White House he left
if not unbowed, then exceedingly unpopular. In fact, he ended his
tenure as one of the most unpopular presidents in American history, with approval ratings a scant 34 percent. Obama's ratings have
all along been higher—particularly in the beginning and then again
immediately following the assassination of Osama bin Laden—but
he too lost traction over time and experienced the kinds of humilia-
tions now routinely endured by leaders in high places.

The Obama administration has had important accomplishments, with health-care legislation, a stimulus program, a nuclear
arms treaty with Russia, and the elimination of bin Laden among
them. However, the costs have been high, not least to the president himself, who routinely has been lambasted by pundits for in
some way falling short, and who was humbled by the electorate just
two years into his presidency. The 2010 midterm elections were a
major political defeat for the White House. The Republicans won
seven new seats in the Senate, as many new governorships, and they
took the seats of 720 Democrats in state legislatures. But the most

significant shift was in the U.S. House of Representatives, where sixty-three districts changed hands, the largest such swing vote since 1932.[7] With the benefit of hindsight it has become blindingly clear that these elections were critical: they were the necessary precursors to the miserable debacle that became the 2011 debt crisis, which, among its other debilitating effects both political and economic, further debased Washington's already diminished leadership class.

This raises a question: has the American presidency become the most impossible job in the world?[8] Apart from the exceedingly difficult context within which the office now is situated, and apart from the recalcitrant cast of characters who ostensibly constitute the president's followers, the office of the president has swollen over the last half century and so has the number of exceedingly difficult problems the president is expected somehow to solve. Changes like these do more to explain our chronic dissatisfaction (save in the wake of a spectacular presidential exploit) with presidential performance than does anything else, including presidential performance per se. And they further explain why even supposedly sympathetic observers are forever finding fault.

Frank Rich, a longtime op-ed columnist for the *New York Times*, now with *New York* magazine, is well known as a liberal Democrat. But a year or two into the Obama presidency, Rich began regularly, relentlessly, and harshly to criticize Obama. Rich wrote at one point that the original Obama was "too hot not to cool down." Then he asked, "But still: How did we get to the nadir so fast?"[9]

Here was the problem as Rich saw it—Obama was a centrist, not a traditional liberal Democrat. As far as the Democratic base was concerned, the president was too measured and too tepid—his long-delayed and becalmed response to the disastrous explosion of the oil drilling rig Deepwater Horizon off the coast of Louisiana in 2010 was considered typical. Of course, to the Republican right as well, Obama's response to the disaster was flawed, though for different reasons. The right attacked Obama for doing too much—for obliging the culprit company, British Petroleum, to set up a $20 billion escrow fund for victims of the spill, which to conservatives only confirmed their belief that a "rank incompetent and closet socialist" had "seized the White House to subvert America and the free-enterprise system."[10]

Eventually the faultfinders came to include Obama himself, who, even before the humiliating midterm elections, knew something had gone wrong. By his own rendering, while he was able to inspire *during* the campaign, he was unable to inspire *after* the campaign was over. In other words, once he was required actually to govern, Obama became aware of how difficult it is to exercise leadership in America—and of his own limitations as a leader. It was a daunting mix: Obama's complete lack of executive experience; the culture of Washington, more prone to resist change than to facilitate it; the American people, now more fickle than loyal, more impatient and entitled than long-suffering; and challenges at home and abroad that were nearly overwhelming.

Ken Duberstein was a top aide to Ronald Reagan who nevertheless disliked George W. Bush and so voted for Obama in 2008. But, after a couple of years of Obama in the White House, Duberstein was disappointed. "When [Obama] talked about being a transformational president, it was about restoring the faith of the American people in our governing institutions. What we now know is that that did not work. If anything, people are even more dubious about all of our institutions, especially government."[11]

People Power

It would appear at first glance our primary response has been acceptance. After all, until the Occupy movement, which gained steam only in autumn 2011, the American people (in contrast to people in other Western democracies) had not marched in the streets to protest, or picketed the White House or any other institution of government. Nor had they regularly sought to impeach elected officials to whom they took serious exception. Even college campuses, traditionally a bastion of rebellion, had generally been quiet. To be sure, all along there were lots of screaming and yelling, lots of griping and complaining and finger-pointing, but in the United States, again, until Occupy Wall Street, most of the griping took place in the wired world rather than in the real world. In spite of all the talk among pundits about "populist rage," there had been no obvious, overt indication of people protesting as there was in, say, the 1960s and '70s.

Several explanations for the apparent passivity have been offered, including individuals being less invested in their communities, the lack of a higher political purpose, cities being less densely crowded than at earlier points in American history, and the Internet, which some have argued saps passion rather than feeds it. As sociologist Sudhir Venkatesh put it, technology "separates us and makes more of our communication indirect, impersonal, and emotionally flat. With headsets on and our hands busily texting, we are less aware of one another's behavior in public space."[12]

But, as we have seen, technology is a double-edged sword. It can separate us or it can bring us together. Social media in particular sometimes makes us *more* aware of what others are thinking and doing—including in "public space." Which brings me to my point: twenty-first-century technology enables domestic political resistance, even political protest, to take different forms. To make my case I cite two examples of people power—the first from the left, the second from the right—that changed the face of American politics. Neither is unfamiliar, but together, seen as political protest in contemporary dress, they give clear evidence that the dubiousness to which Duberstein alludes has in fact inspired and incited ordinary people to take political action. They give clear evidence that followers, ordinary Americans, are not lacking in power or influence.

The first example is the election of Barack Obama as president of the United States, which was, in fact, a shock. It was an event that, just a few years earlier, was inconceivable. Obama came out of nowhere to upend American politics by dethroning the then queen of the Democratic Party—Hillary Clinton.

Obviously Clinton is a woman, which in a campaign for the American presidency was, is, still considered a liability. But in every other aspect her path to the White House, or, at least to her nomination for president, seemed secure. Among other reasons, there was no competition. There were others in the running for the Democratic ticket, of course, but none with a demonstrable interest in the job had the national name recognition, political experience, and financial resources to mount a credible challenge to Clinton, who, as former first lady and then senator from New York, was in every obvious way the front-runner. Almost no one, including Barack Obama himself, imagined him taking on Clinton, at least not at first. As John Heilemann and Mark Halperin wrote in their bestselling chronicle of the campaign, *Game Change*, Obama "was all too aware that he was still just a freshman [senator] and therefore at the beck and call of his party's leadership."[13]

However, several senior Democrats were edgy about Clinton's candidacy. They wanted a winner, a nominee who could take the White House back from the Republicans, and they were not convinced that Clinton was the best the Democrats could do. Her negative ratings were high, she remained a polarizing figure, and her husband, former president Bill Clinton, could not be relied on to behave impeccably. So in 2006, Senate Majority Leader Harry Reid summoned Obama to his office to suggest that he might plausibly challenge Hillary Clinton for the Democratic nomination for president of the United States.

Again, now that Obama has been president for some time, it is hard to recall the extent to which this scenario seemed implausible. Obama lacked Clinton's name recognition; he had scant political experience of any sort; and he had almost no money with which to mount a credible campaign against so formidable an opponent. In addition, both Clinton and her husband considered her nomination a given. According to Heilemann and Halperin, "The Clintons saw themselves as the party's de facto First Family. . . . As the only Democrats in recent memory who had demonstrated a consistent capacity to win national elections. As revered and beloved figures." So when things got to the point where Obama had the temerity to snag an all-important early primary victory in Iowa, Bill Clinton was left "red-faced and simmering," while Hillary Clinton was reduced to being "bitter and befuddled." As mind-boggling as Obama's Iowa victory was, it did suggest that a young black man, unknown and untested, could possibly become president of the United States.[14]

Though some senior Democrats, Reid most prominent among them, gave Obama early succor, the fact that he clobbered first Clinton and then, in the general election, John McCain, was a different sort of triumph altogether. It was a triumph by and large of outsiders over insiders (that is, over most of the Democratic establishment), of young over old, of newly engaged black voters over traditional white voters, of grassroots power over positional power, and of new media over old media. Obama's stupefying series of successes during 2008 was evidence of the newfound clout of ordinary people, of followers not willing any longer to be Bystanders—and more than willing, eager even, to be Participants and Activists.[15] It is this kind of transfer of power and influence from the apparently strong to the apparently weak that in the twenty-first century is especially significant. And it is this kind of transfer that the leadership industry often fails carefully and consistently even to consider.

A key component of Obama's campaign was his use of new media, which left both Clinton and McCain in the dust. With regard to money, Obama did the impossible: first, he declined public funding and then he broke all previous fund-raising records. How? He turned to the Internet to raise half his money from ordinary Americans, in increments of less than two hundred dollars. With regard to organization, Obama did essentially the same: his campaign used technology to transform Isolates and Bystanders into Participants and Activists.[16] Put in terms I use here, Obama's campaign staff had a level of contextual intelligence unmatched by the opposition. They understood two important things that their opponents did not: that the culture had changed, and that the plethora of new media was a game changer. Again, this was an evolution (or information revolution) that in retrospect seems obvious. But the McCain campaign was stuck in the past, unable to adapt to the new and different.

The Tea Party, which was started only in 2009, is testimony that plain people on the right, like plain people on the left, will not be stilled. Mark Lilla called the Tea Party a "libertarian eruption"—it deliberately evoked America's revolutionary history and it was prompted by several plaints, not least among them the fact that Barack Obama was in the White House.[17]

The Tea Party is not, as some would have it, a simple artifact of conservative and corporate interests. To the contrary: while they, like other American ideologues, are funded by the rich, Tea Partiers themselves tend not to belong to any elite. Fewer than half are college graduates and only a quarter earn over $100,000. In fact, the Tea Party is the product of a genuine grassroots movement that tapped into both antigovernment populism and the widespread distrust not just of government, but of all the establishments Americans once admired unquestioningly.[18] In addition, it has been a genuinely leaderless movement, or, if you prefer, a movement with many lesser leaders in many different places, not one of whom has achieved national name recognition through the Tea Party alone. This is not to say that big money, big media, and big names have no place in the Tea Party—they do, again, like everywhere else in American politics. Yet the movement is indeed composed largely of those I call followers, middle-class and, yes, white Americans, who are by most accounts ordinary people organizing around issues that energize and motivate them, and what they consider to be their best interests.

In 2008 Amy Kremer and Jenny Beth Martin were, according to the *Wall Street Journal*, "30-something suburbanites in metro Atlanta, frustrated by recession, dismayed by the election of Barack Obama, and waiting for the next chapter of their lives." By early 2009, these two had helped to found the first major national organization in the Tea Party movement. For his part, Michael Patrick Leahy, an otherwise unremarkable technology consultant from Nashville, was similarly riled by the usual party politics, so he decided to contribute to the Tea Party his particular skill set, which was new media.

Once again technology played a key role—arguably *the* key role. It connected people like Kremer, Martin, and Leahy early on, thus enabling the Tea Party to get off to a running start. By first developing and then expanding the Tea Party's new media savvy, a man like Leahy was able to have an immediate impact on right-wing American politics—and so was a woman like Stacy Mott, a stay-at-home mother of three young children who started a blog for conservative women (Smart Girl Politics) and soon signed on with Kremer and Martin. So it was that the Tea Party movement snowballed—more and more people making more and more connections, primarily but not exclusively online, and soon getting to critical mass. Before long, Tea Party activists had joined old political tactics (rallies, protests) to new political tactics (email blasts, blogs), thereby creating out of whole cloth a force in American politics with which both the right and the left had no choice but to reckon.[19]

None of this is to say that the Tea Party will prove enduring, that it will for years to come have an impact on American political discourse, or on the outcomes of elections. It is quite possible, in fact, that the very speed and ease with which it made its presence felt will make the Tea Party "more ephemeral and less transformative."[20] Similarly, it is quite possible that there will eventually be competition—another such movement on the right, or on the left, a product perhaps of Occupy Wall Street, that will give Tea Partiers a run for their money. In fact, it has already been argued that in the months before the 2012 elections, the Tea Party is "increasingly swimming against the tide of public opinion."[21]

But whatever the future of the Tea Party, of its short past this can already be said: its effects have been transformative. It has recast the political debate by putting the country's fiscal problems front and center, and it brought Washington nearly to a standstill and the nation to the brink of default. It further confirmed the following: that ordinary Americans potentially have vast political power and influence, particularly in the twenty-first century; that ordinary Americans have the capacity in the twenty-first century to organize with remarkable alacrity; that technology has changed forever the way American politics is played; that an impassioned minority can bend a becalmed majority; that leaders in high places can be bled by followers who refuse to follow; and that in twenty-first-century America the new and different can nearly immediately impinge on the tried and true.

Not incidentally, the Tea Party was initially credited with reviving the Republican Party, which in 2009 was, as Peter Boyer writes, "battered and exhausted."[22] In fact, John Boehner, the Ohio Republican who became Speaker of the House in January 2011, said it was Tea Partiers who obliged Republicans to rebrand in a way that otherwise would have taken a generation to achieve. Why? Because among other reasons, when the 112th Congress convened in January 2011, fully one-third of Republican members were freshmen who to some degree identified with the Tea Party movement.

But as things turned out, Tea Partiers proved difficult if not actually impossible for a more centrist, establishment Republican like Boehner to lead. The Speaker did what he could: he campaigned for Tea Partiers, moved millions from his own campaign chest to theirs, adopted some of their rhetoric, and gave them a seat at the leadership table. He shifted his own political positions to accommodate theirs, and he tried every which way to minimize the differences between mainstream Republicans like himself and the Tea Partiers to his right. In other words, the man did everything he knew how to win over and placate his recalcitrant followers. Nevertheless, his considerable efforts were mostly in vain. The evidence suggests—evidence that during the debt crisis grew sky high—that Speaker Boehner had more trouble with his own followers, with members of his own party, than he did with the Democratic opposition. Still, give the Tea Partiers credit where credit is due. Certainly in this situation, they bent to their will not only Republican leaders, but Democratic ones as well, including the nation's chief executive.

Finally, there is Occupy Wall Street—which with the benefit of hindsight will be judged the inevitable product of cumulated grievances, of a national breakdown perceived by many to be political as well as economic. As we will see in the next chapter, for years now followers have protested inequities the world over—Americans were, in other words, late to the twenty-first-century protest party. But once Occupy Wall Street was joined, it took on a life of its own, spreading with the alacrity that technology now allows, using populist rhetoric to engage the young and restless, the disaffected and unemployed, the alienated and angry, the disenchanted, disillusioned, and disappointed.

After its obscure start—it was started by Adbusters, a Vancouver-based group inspired by the Arab Spring—in just a few weeks Occupy Wall Street was able to claim the following: that its grass-roots movement represented 99 percent of the American people (in opposition to the 1 percent that controlled America's wealth); that its campaign had spread to 1,500 cities worldwide and 100 cities nationwide; that it had brought to its knees, if only briefly and intermittently, the city of New York; and that it had begun to take on bastions of Wall Street such as JPMorgan Chase. (Chase defended itself, pointing out it had repaid the $25 billion borrowed from the government, and hired 13,000 people in the third quarter of 2011, including 2,000 veterans.)

Tellingly, significantly, certainly for the leadership industry, Occupy Wall Street made it a point to claim what other such groups have similarly claimed: that it was "leaderless." Put differently, leadership, which for the last several decades has been so famously in fashion, is now, at least in some circles, out of fashion. From day one Occupy Wall Street insisted that it had no clear hierarchy, that it had many leaders and no leaders, and that "there's power over, power under, and power within. We're trying to get rid of power over."[23]

Compromised Corporate Corpus

A specter is haunting corporate America. The specter is of hunger, of leaders and managers looking for more and more money and power at the expense of the rest. This is not to say that corporate executives do a bad job or get no respect—to the contrary. By and large they perform well, and by and large they are envied and emulated. Still, something's off, something's gone wrong in recent years—the economy generally, high unemployment particularly, with leaders in business getting much of the blame.

What accounts for this mix of envy and disdain directed at those at the apex of American business? The first reason involves a trend now decades in duration: the gap between rich and poor has steadily increased, and the size of the middle class has steadily decreased. The second reason is the financial crisis, the worst since the Depression, from which the United States has yet to recover. The third is that business leaders now resemble political leaders—their names and faces are familiar, if not famous. Inclined no longer to hide behind a corporate curtain, able no longer to remain anonymous in gray flannel suits and executive suites, the captains of industry are now known to many Americans, especially aficionados of finance fed endless information by new media and old, 24/7. Rick Wagoner, former CEO of General Motors, became the symbol of the decline and near disappearance of the American auto industry, just as surely as Lloyd Blankfein, CEO of Goldman Sachs, came to embody the excesses of financial services—and, for that matter, just as surely as Bill Gates and Steve Jobs, of Microsoft and Apple respectively, came to incarnate the best of American innovation. Finally, there is the impression of widespread corporate corruption without commensurate corporate punishment. The result is a cadre of corporate leaders who, though amply rewarded financially, are widely disliked and distrusted.

A 2011 Gallup poll confirmed that corporate America is in disrepute. A large majority of Americans (62 percent) want major corporations to have less influence in the future than they do at present, up 10 percent from a decade earlier. Additionally, corporate America is considered too powerful: fully 67 percent of those polled said they resented the influence of big business. It's got to the point where even Republicans, historically friendlier to business than Democrats, are skeptics. Only 13 percent of Republicans believe major corporations should have more influence in the future than they do in the present.[24] Even Fox News, known as right of center, was obliged to confirm the increasingly obvious. When it conducted a poll on whether certain individuals and institutions were helping or hurting the economy, the lowest score went to corporate chief executives. By almost six to one, those surveyed said corporate leaders had done more to hurt than help the economy—a rating worse than the president or even congress.[25]

Between 2002 and 2007, the bottom 99 percent of American incomes grew 1.3 percent a year, while the incomes of the top 1 percent grew 10 percent. This 1 percent accounted for two-thirds of all income growth in those years. Moreover, even within this top 1 percent, incomes became more concentrated. Based on these numbers, financial columnist James Surowiecki provides additional grist for the mill: "So at the same time that the rich have been pulling away from the middle class, the very rich have been pulling away from the pretty rich, and the very, very rich have been pulling away from the very rich."[26]

Executive pay has become, for obvious reasons, a target.[27] It does not soothe our savage breasts to learn that near the depths of the recent recession, in 2008, Larry Ellison, CEO of Oracle, received nearly $193 million in total compensation; Daniel Amos, CEO of Aflac, received more than $75 million; and Steven Burd, CEO of Safeway, received $67 million.[28] Nor does it help to discover that the median pay for top executives at two hundred big companies in 2010 was $10.8 million, a 23 percent jump from 2009; and that big bucks are being shelled out even to corporate leaders who perform poorly. In 2010, *Bloomberg Businessweek* estimated that a good number of prominent CEOs—for example, Antonio Perez, who failed to turn around Eastman Kodak—were being vastly overpaid, in Perez's case by some 278 percent.[29] A year later, when Leo Apotheker, CEO of Hewlett-Packard for less than twelve months, was shown the door by the board, he was paid for his pains to the tune of more than $13.2 million—in addition to the $10 million he had recently received just for signing on. Gannett's CEO, Craig Dubow, stayed six years; but his tenure was described by David Carr in the *New York Times* as "a disaster." Still, when he resigned, he left with $37.1 million in retirement and benefits—plus the $16 million he was paid two years previously.[30]

Executive compensation became a focal point because of institutional problems that in addition to pay, included tying incentives to risk taking, particularly in financial services, and the lack of corporate checks and balances to constrain corporate governance. Still, most of the complaints were about pay as an indicator of unfairness. Nobel Prize–winning economist Joseph Stiglitz put it this way: "The upper 1 percent of Americans are now taking in nearly a quarter of the nation's income every year."[31] (It is from Stiglitz that Occupy Wall Street got its slogan, "We are the 99 percent.")

There have been similar problems at the individual level, with corporate leaders who in general are not so much considered ineffective as unethical, or, at least, greedy to the point of unseemly. The complaint against leaders in business is not only that they became

excessively rich, but that they did so while so many others strug-
gled, are struggling, to make ends meet. And the divide between the
haves and have-nots is not only about money. It is also about class
and lifestyle and values. This is not to say the revolution is at hand—
hardly. There is no hard evidence that the American people are
prepared on any massive scale to protest capitalism in its current
incarnation. But there is widespread pessimism—and a recurring
refrain about the disappearing American Dream.[32]

So the situation in business is different from the situation in
government. In government we have leaders who are perceived by
and large as unable to do what they are supposed to do, to lead. In
business we have leaders who are perceived by and large as able to
do what they are supposed to do, to lead, but who nevertheless do so
in ways that disappoint and dishearten. This is an important distinction, one not usually made by the leadership industry, which
tends anyway to accentuate the positive and eliminate the negative,
and to teach how to lead as if one size fits all. To be sure, leading in
government is not altogether different from leading in business. In
fact, good leaders in one sector are likely as not to be good leaders in
another. Still there are differences, some of which are important.

The complaints against leaders in the private sector, again,
especially in financial services, are many in number, though not
so many in kind. President Obama branded Wall Street bankers
"shameful" for giving themselves nearly $20 billion in bonuses
as the economy was deteriorating and the government was spending billions to bail out their businesses. Researchers at the International Monetary Fund warned that "a rare opportunity is being
thrown away to tackle the underlying causes" of the global financial meltdown, because financial institutions are not restructuring
their ways of doing business.[33] And others took note of the fact that
in apportioning blame for the financial crisis, "corporate boards of

directors have remained remarkably unscathed, even though they effectively approved the strategies that immolated so many companies."[34]

Academics have charged that CEOs can be narcissistic to the point of being dysfunctional. "All people, especially leaders," noted leadership expert Manfred Kets de Vries, "need a healthy dose of narcissism . . . it's the engine that drives leadership." But if the narcissism is extreme, leaders lose touch, while those around them typically are, as we have seen repeatedly throughout human history, unwilling or unable to apply corrective measures.[35] Others have similarly warned of what one referred to as "the modern cult of the heroic chief executive," cautioning against domineering leaders who fill their boards with their supporters (think Rupert Murdoch), and are enabled by advisers and analysts interested mainly in their own well-being.[36]

Still other experts find that leaders are not only less important than *they* imagine, but also less important than *we* imagine. One found that although we have "this almost blind belief that the manager at the top changes everything," in fact he or she generally does not. This is not to argue that CEOs are insignificant. It is to argue that since "changes in leadership account for [only] roughly 10% of the variance in corporate profitability on average," they are not omnipotent.[37] Of course my own view on this is that we, particularly those of us in the leadership industry, tend over and over again to make the leader attribution error: to assume the leader is where the action is. Though in exceptional cases—the iconic Steve Jobs again comes to mind—this holds true, more often than not it doesn't.

Finally, there are numberless attacks on individual CEOs, singled out for their abysmal professional performance. Such attacks are directed not only at obvious candidates for tarring and feathering such as James Cayne, onetime CEO of now-defunct Bear

Stearns, and Richard Fuld, onetime CEO of now-defunct Lehman Brothers. They are directed as well at less obvious targets, such as Jeffrey Immelt, CEO of General Electric, who whatever else his accomplishments has proved his staying power, and James Dimon, CEO of JPMorgan Chase, one of the few top bankers to emerge from the recession with his reputation more or less intact. Immelt was embarrassed by a *Bloomberg Businessweek* story titled "Can GE Still Manage?" The charge, in a nutshell, was incompetence: "CEO Jeff Immelt says his company trains the best business leaders in the world. Yet they haven't saved him from a hellish decade that cut GE's value in half."[38] Dimon, meanwhile, was raked over the coals by Graydon Carter, editor of *Vanity Fair*, who suggested arrogance to the point of outrageousness. Carter attacked Dimon for trying to "elevate himself above his fellow bankers," to frame himself as a thinker and a statesman. "You have to admire the fellow's ambitions," Carter carped; "making the rounds trying to drum up sympathy for a group of people whose unregulated betting parlors drove governments and businesses into the ground, along the way leaving untold millions without work around the world . . . is no easy task."[39]

Whether justified or not, attacks like these signal a time in which business leaders, like political leaders, are considered fair game. This applies in spades to bad leaders, to failed, flawed CEOs who are by now thought to be so many in number there is occasionally the impression they are not the exception but rather the rule. As Carter complained, many who were too greedy have managed to escape unscathed. Add to this the media's (new media and old) voracious appetite for bad news about bad people, and our own insatiable curiosity about the high and mighty who fall far fast, and you have explained our fixation on those who did wrong. Small wonder so many think the problem is not just a few rotten apples, but in fact whole bushels of them.

But are they far wrong? What we do know for certain is this: in spite of our obsession with ethics (triggered by the collapse of Enron), ethics courses and ethics trainings, codes of ethics and ethics officers—the evidence of corporate corruption or, at least, of corner-cutting for profit-making, continues to be widespread. One representative survey of America's largest corporations in the 1990s found that two-thirds had been involved in illegal activities during the ten years preceding.[40] Add to this the constant accounts of corruption—Tyson Foods, for example, agreed to pay the U.S. government millions of dollars in fines and other penalties for allowing its Mexican chicken plants to bribe inspectors, though no heads ever rolled as a result of the infractions.[41] And add in the long lists of "worst managers"—"some who helped set the economic crisis in motion; others [who] managed to make a bad situation worse," and leaders who are either famously incompetent, miserably immoral, or both.[42] Think of Tony Hayward, for example, erstwhile CEO of British Petroleum, who, along with his predecessor, John Browne, ignored "omens of disaster," signs of coming calamity long before that massive oil leak in the Gulf of Mexico. This is not even to speak of Hayward after the crisis, which he had handled so poorly, the board had virtually no choice but to sack him immediately. What does the leadership industry have to say about this? What does it have to say about the fact that even after all the recent efforts at teaching ethics, particularly in schools of business, the goal—corporate leaders who are demonstrably more ethical than their predecessors—continues to elude us? Not much, or at least not much that is substantive.

As for all those Wall Street bankers—CEOs astride financial services companies—where to begin? Together they tarnished an entire industry for years to come. Together they became synonymous with the aggrandizement of money and power at the expense of those with none of either. Together they came to symbolize a system in which those who do wrong escape not only unscathed, but enriched. And together they threw into question nothing less than the efficacy *and* the fairness of American capitalism.

Take the case of John Thain. His career was "charmed" and his pedigree impeccable. He was "the Clark Kent of Wall Street," an apparently "mild-mannered executive with a square jaw and glasses who had kept 'Mother Merrill' [Merrill Lynch] from following Lehman Brothers into bankruptcy." But once the house of cards came down, it was revealed that in an attempt to save Merrill, Thain had sold billions of dollars of soured investments for pennies on the dollar; that his frantic attempt to stave off disaster was itself a disaster; that he had renovated his office to the tune of $1.2 million; that he was volatile to the point of heaving furniture against a wall; and that just before he was shown the door he paid $4 billion in bonuses to Merrill executives.[43]

At least Angelo Mozilo had to pay the piper—something. In fact, according to the *New York Times*, Mozilo was the first prominent chief executive to be "held personally accountable for questionable business practices that contributed to the housing bubble, the dizzying financial machinations that surrounded it, and a ruinous lending spree that ultimately threatened to undermine the nation's economy."[44] In 2008, Mozilo, CEO of Countrywide Financial, the nation's largest mortgage lender, received $102.84 million in total compensation. Two years later he was obliged to settle civil securities fraud and insider trading charges against him—albeit without having to admit to wrongdoing or having to serve a day in jail. Moreover, while he did have to pay $67.5 million in a penalty and reparations to investors, and he was permanently banned from serving as an officer or director of a public company, $20 million of his fine was paid by Countrywide, and the remainder was a fraction of his somehow self-made fortune—estimated to be more than $600 million.

The story of the meltdown is nearly over—but not completely. For example, in 2011 the Federal Deposit Insurance Corporation sued three top executives of Washington Mutual, including CEO Kerry Killinger, seeking to hold them responsible for enriching themselves while going on a "lending spree, knowing that the real estate market was in a 'bubble.'" Additionally, two of their wives were similarly sued; the claim stated that they had illegally moved cash and houses into trusts to protect their assets from legal claims. What exactly went wrong in this instance? It was not for lack of knowing—top officials at WaMu knew perfectly well the housing market was at historically high risk. Still they continued to lend because their role model was none other than Countrywide Financial—which meant that if they did *not* lend, they would lose market share, thereby cutting their own compensation. So it happened that, as one senator put it, WaMu became a model of "corporate ineptitude, greed, and wrongdoing."[15] (Some months later the case against Killinger and colleagues was settled; it cost them, but only a fraction of what the government originally sought.)

Deadlock

President Obama has not magically changed much of anything. Nor has the Tea Party, or for that matter the Occupy movement. Similarly, the private sector, for all its sometime successes, is so self-interested it simply cannot be, in and of itself, the solution to a significant national problem.

So the United States is stuck in a rut. Too many leaders are unwilling or unable to lead effectively and ethically. And too many followers are unable to figure out how reasonably to respond, such as joining together to form a third party, to give just one example. (A new political start-up, Americans Elect, is determined to use the Internet to do just that, to identify a third, viable, centrist candidate for president in 2012. But if history is any guide, the prospects for such a candidate remain dim, at least for now.) In addition, the context is more daunting than it is anything else, nearly overwhelming in its complexity and in the magnitude of its challenges. In short, neither government nor business, nor any single individual or institution, seems up to curing what ails us—whether unemployment, the national debt, failing schools, affordable health care, climate change, nuclear proliferation, deteriorating infrastructure—you name it.

Washington, it is said, is "suicidal."[46] Our political leaders are "paralyzed by the very thought of asking constituents to make short-term sacrifices for long term rewards"—and we ourselves are too entitled.[47] Furthermore, institutions across the board are in precipitous decline: "Nearly every pillar institution in American society—whether it's General Motors, Congress, Wall Street, Major League Baseball, the Catholic Church or the mainstream media—[has in recent years] revealed itself to be corrupt, incompetent or both."[48] Things have got to a point where democracy itself seems vulnerable, open, for perhaps the first time ever in American history, to question. "So now we have a country," wrote Kurt Andersen, that is "absolutely teeming with irregular passions and artful misrepresentations, whipped up to an unprecedented pitch and volume by the fundamentally new means of 24/7 cable and the hyperdemocratic web."[49]

The result of all this is a level of disappointment and distrust that threatens to undermine or even undo what has been the singular self-confidence of the American people. Leading in America has never been easy. But now it is more difficult than ever—not only because we have too many *bad leaders*, but because we have too many *bad followers*. Many of us don't vote at all, or vote along strict or even extreme ideological lines, making it hard for *political* leaders to do what they *must*—to collaborate to compromise. And many of us are too timid, too alienated, and/or, too disorganized to speak up and speak out, making it easy for corporate leaders to do what they *want*—to do what's best for them and their bank accounts. Whatever it is that ails us, in other words, is not only about those at the top falling down on the job, but also about those in the middle and at the bottom falling down on theirs.

6

Worldwide Momentum—
upgrading followers

Whatever the changes at home—the slow but certain deterioration in the status of leaders—they have been superseded by changes abroad. It would be difficult to exaggerate the extent of the differences between what many, if not most, countries in Europe, Asia, Africa, and Latin America were only three or four decades ago, and what they are in the present. Across large swaths of the globe there have been seismic shifts in relations between leaders and followers, with most, though not all, leaving the first weaker and the second stronger. However, unlike the American experience, in which the balance shifted on account of the diminished leader, the balance worldwide shifted on account of the enhanced, and in many cases, the emboldened, follower.

Closing the *Black Book of Communism*—Russia and China

One of the defining geopolitical trends of the last twenty-five years has been the spread of democracy. In 1975, 30 nations of the world had governments that were popularly elected. By 2005 that number had climbed to 119.[1] Since then, the growth of democracy has slowed or stopped in some countries, including Bangladesh, Venezuela, Nigeria, and Philippines. And in others, such as Egypt and Tunisia, it is not so far robust (though in 2011 Tunisia had peaceful free elections).[2] Still, conditions conducive to democracy—modernization, for example—are nearly everywhere in evidence, which is why political participation by ordinary people has grown to levels previously inconceivable.[3]

In some cases, the once powerless wanted equity above all—in South Africa, for example, which in the early 1990s transitioned, finally, from apartheid to majority rule. In other cases, the change from old order to new centered on the disappearing communist dictator. Dictators still exist, of course, but their realm has shrunk in recent years and is shrinking still. Additionally, in place of the dictator in countries such as Russia and China is a leadership cadre that is obliged to consider in its calculations characters that include, among others, the people themselves.

Though estimates vary, under the rule of Joseph Stalin, *because* of the rule of Joseph Stalin, some 20 million people in the Soviet Union died. And, though estimates vary, the number of Chinese deaths attributed to Mao Zedong during the Great Leap Forward *alone*, from 1958 to 1962, is generally thought to have been about 45 million, all worked, starved, or beaten to death.[4] These sorts of numbers repeat themselves in other former communist countries, which is a testament not only to man's inhumanity toward man, but to our own vulnerability to being debased or even destroyed by those more powerful than we.[5]

How did the collapse of communism, the demise of the dictator, come to pass? At the *macro* level it was a combination of repressed political aspirations, depressed economic conditions, and growing dissent—Participants, Activists, and some brave Diehards, unwilling any longer meekly to follow.[6] And, at the *micro* level, it was a series of events that began with the death of the tyrant (Stalin died in 1953 and Mao in 1976) and extended, first in the Soviet Union and Eastern Europe, then later in China, to gradual, moderate, systemic relaxation.

The Soviet Union began to change soon after Stalin died, when he was taken to task by one of his successors, Nikita Khrushchev. After Khrushchev's death, the Soviet Union started to stagnate, while voices of dissent—such as the late, great Andrei Sakharov, along with his wife, Elena Bonner, and Aleksandr Solzhenitsyn—grew louder and clearer and greater in number. Finally, in the late 1980s, not long after President Mikhail Gorbachev publicly confirmed that the Soviet experience was other than utopian, an iconic event in modern history took place: the fall of the Berlin Wall.[7] In its immediate aftermath came the collapse of communism, first in the Soviet bloc and then in that bastion of communism, the Soviet Union itself.

In China, the story is in some ways similar and in others different. China began to normalize and modernize under Deng Xiaoping, supreme leader for about a decade and a half, beginning in the late 1970s. Under Deng, China remained a communist state, but the conception of what constituted communism was expanded, eventually becoming market authoritarianism. Put another way, China became a powerhouse economically, while keeping the lid on politically. China is not, obviously, a liberal democracy—any more than is Russia. Still, in making the transition from totalitarianism to authoritarianism, China's leaders freed more followers in more ways than ever before.

To be sure, all of this is relative. Ordinary people in both Russia and China are still muzzled, not free by a long shot to do or say what they want when they want, or to select either their system of governance or their governors. But here is the important point: given that their recent histories were stained by dismal dictatorships, both Russia and China have come very far very fast. In spite of their history—scant knowledge of democratic theory and no experience with democratic practice—leaders and followers in both Russia and China have been transformed. In fact, in nearly all of the formerly communist countries, there has been a sea change in relations between leaders and followers. The former have evolved from tyrants to autocrats or even democrats, and the latter from being hideously oppressed to being something less—repressed. These changes constituted one of the more dramatic transformations in human history. And they signaled the beginning of an era, the last couple of decades of the twentieth century, in which leaders around the world were reduced, while followers were enhanced. Similarly, they foretold a time in which the study of leadership was no longer in and of itself sufficient. Even from a purely intellectual or theoretical perspective, it is no longer possible to understand Russia or China by understanding only one man, or even what just a generation or two ago was referred to as the political elite.

Changing and Staying the Same—Russia and China

In the last several decades, the questions remained the same: How can Russia and China get from here to there, from totalitarianism to authoritarianism, without sacrificing leaders on the altar of their followers? How can Russia and China encourage transformative *economic* progress without allowing transformative *political* progress?

While Russia and China are, as suggested, more different than they are similar, as far as patterns of dominance and deference are concerned, the similarities between them are neither incidental nor unimportant. In both Russia and China the tradition of having a single political strongman continues to the present day—and this person tends to prevail for a long period of time. However, the following factors pertain to both countries as well. First, this strongman is now beholden to and dependent on others. Second, ordinary people are straining to have their say. Third, government officials remain vigilant about maintaining political control. Fourth, there is one set of rules for how to behave in the political realm, and another set of rules for how to behave in the economic one. Fifth, change is being driven by culture and technology. And, finally, there is contagion—people aware of events elsewhere in the world and, in turn, affected by their awareness.

Russia's leaders are beset by followers who refuse to shut up. The Kremlin still stifles the opposition: neither under strongman (and prime minister) Vladimir Putin nor under his successor as president, Dmitri Medvedev, have protests been allowed beyond a certain point. But the fact that there is any resistance at all in Russia is indicative.

Most of the recent protests seemed on the surface to be insignificant, but they were not. Their impact was cumulative: angry motorists mustering some of Moscow's largest demonstrations in years to protest high gas prices, bad roads, and corrupt police; environmentalists risking arrest as they attempted to stop construction of a road along a forest near the Russian capital; gay rights activists protesting in Moscow in spite of a ban against their public displays; protests in Moscow, St. Petersburg, Kaliningrad, and Vladivostok against government officials planning to raise tariffs on second-hand foreign cars; a 10,000-person protest in Kaliningrad against an unpopular governor; and terrorism, the response of last resort by Muslims living under semifeudalism in some of Russia's eighty-three provinces and autonomous regions. In fact, occasionally there was dissent even at the highest levels. When it was announced that Putin planned to return as president in 2012, not only did his approval ratings rapidly decline among the Russian people, but Russia's finance minister, Aleksei Kudrin, declared that he at least would not be willing to serve in the next government. Finally, in late 2011, there was an astonishing explosion of public protest. Twice over, tens of thousands of Muscovites took to the streets to challenge Putin's power.

Russia's leaders are caught between modernity on the one hand—including rising expectations and growing demands—and chaos and repression on the other. The *Wall Street Journal* describes their dilemma: "The prospect of further unrest poses what could be the biggest challenge yet to the authoritarian system built by Mr. Putin. It also foists a stark choice on the Kremlin: to stifle dissent, or to placate protesters to provide some kind of pressure outlet."[8]

Aleksei Navalny is a sign of the times. Navalny is a lawyer by training, based in Moscow, whose website reaches between one and two million people a day. While his website was originally intended to expose corruption in business, more recently he has exposed corruption in government—sometimes to great effect. In fact, when Navalny charged fraud to the tune of $4 billion in the case of Transneft, a state-run pipeline company, Putin himself was obliged to call for an investigation. Again, caution is in order. Putin shows his enemies no mercy, as in the infamous case of Mikhail Khodorkovsky, who in less than a decade went from being Russia's richest man to being its most prominent political prisoner. (Khodorkovsky made the near-fatal mistake of becoming politically active and backing Putin's opponents.) Moreover, Russia's most enterprising journalists, lawyers, and muckrakers all have had hard times in recent years, with some of the best and bravest beaten and even murdered under circumstances that suggested government involvement. But because the levels of fraud, bribery, and outright theft in Russia are so famously high, Navalny has had some leeway.[9] And by now he has a network in place. If anything happens to him, his work will continue.[10]

In fact, Navalny was arrested during the late 2011 spate of protests. But in silent tribute to his extraordinary influence, he was released from prison after only fifteen days.

China is an even more striking example of the tension between leaders still intent on commanding and controlling, and followers increasingly refusing to fall into line.

Not long ago, we in the West focused on how "un-Communist [China] was becoming."[11] But the Party remains surprisingly vital: it influences China's theory of history, and its political, economic, and military practice. Ian Johnson writes that though many of the Party's policies are not Communist, it is still "Leninist in structure and organization, resulting in institutions and behavior patterns that would be recognizable to leaders of the Russian Revolution." Additionally the Party runs the government—it exercises behind-the-scenes control over those officially in charge. In fact, the Party makes its presence felt in every sector of society, including the law, with judges translating decisions made by the Communist Party into legal rulings.

Finally, instead of simply privatizing the economy, the government has turned state-owned enterprises into shareholder-owned companies in which the government holds a controlling stake. And Chinese companies are run jointly—by CEOs *and* Party secretaries. As Johnson points out, in all the big questions, "party meetings precede board meetings, which largely give routine approval to Party decisions."

Withal, in the last decade, China has been characterized by rapidly rising expectations—especially among the young and restless. They are more highly educated and ambitious than the generations that preceded them, they are more demanding, and they are fluent in the technologies that connect them to like-minded others. Even young Chinese factory workers are less willing than they once were to toil long hours for appallingly low wages. The resulting labor disputes, which in the past were nearly unheard of, have become fairly frequent. As one young labor activist put it, "We're different from our parents' generation. Their wishes were simple—earn some money and return to their hometowns. We want to stay in the cities and enjoy our lives here. But we demand respect."[12]

For a time such unrest—which included a string of worker suicides, sit-ins by white-collar workers, and truckers clashing with the police—was met by a government comparatively willing to make concessions. As recently as 2010, at the Chinese Communist Party's annual plenum there was talk of political reform: the central government would cede some power to local authorities; new laws would be enacted to protect against poor workplace conditions; a system of arbitration would be established; and raises would be given, in some cases to exceed 30 percent. In other words, during the first decade of the twenty-first century the Chinese Communist Party apparently concluded that carefully contained unrest was a safety valve of sorts, precluding further unrest.

This relatively high degree of freedom to protest was accompanied by a relatively high degree of freedom to access the Internet. But China's leaders also feared a future that combined continuing competition from abroad (political, economic, military, and ideological) with increased resistance to authority and access to technology at home. Among other things, we now know (through WikiLeaks) that China's leaders have been wary of technology for years, to the point of being "nearly obsessed with the threat posed by the Internet to their grip on power."[13]

So while China remained relatively repressed even during the last decade (after all, Liu Xiaobo, writer and activist and winner of the 2010 Nobel Peace Prize, has been imprisoned since 2009, serving an eleven-year sentence for inciting state subversion), it was the Arab Spring that made it revert back to being more oppressed. Fearful the unrest might spread—fearful of anything that might hint at a "Jasmine Revolution"—China's leaders stepped in and clamped down, hard. First was a major address by President Hu Jintao on social stability, in which he made three main points: information had to be more tightly controlled; the "virtual society" had to be more tightly regulated; and public opinion had to be guided in different, "healthy directions." This was followed by heightened security: restrictions on activists; more arrests and detainments of dissidents, including Ai Weiwei, an artist of international repute (he was later released); and heightened policing of cell phone calls and other modes of communication, including of course all Internet activity.[14] Reported one researcher, "The crackdown has been the most severe we've seen in years."[15]

Russia and China have changed forever. But they remain in many ways the same—repressive rather than progressive. So the key question is, can their leaders hold down their followers indefinitely? I would argue no: the nature of leadership and followership are so dramatically different from before that extreme, extended repression in countries that are developed is simply not possible. None of this is to say that democratic liberalism is in Russia's future, or for that matter in China's. Rather, it is to make the point that without controlling by resorting to brutality, followers in modernizing countries can no longer be completely stifled or suppressed, at least not indefinitely.

Elsewhere in Europe

People protest all across Europe. Still, France might be considered the poster child for political dissent—a country where followers have long made miserable the lives of their leaders. To the French, resistance is a thing to be cherished and supported, not denounced and suppressed.

As good a place to start as any is France's national soccer team—the same team that traveled to South Africa in 2010 for the World Cup games with a new motto, "All Together for a New Dream." Though on paper it was one of the best in the world, the team played badly in Johannesburg, resulting in all of the following: one top player was sent home for insulting his coach and refusing to apologize; the fitness coach stalked off the field because of a confrontation with a player; players resisted their coaches by refusing even to practice; the team captain claimed there was a traitor on the team; the general manager of the French soccer federation quit South Africa in disgust and flew back to Paris; French newspapers called French players "deserters"; and the French foreign minister described the fiasco as "pathetic"—which, of course, it was. It was also emblematic.

In the recent past the French have verbally mauled their president, Nicolas Sarkozy, alleging that among his other sins he had procured illicit campaign cash from a billionaire heiress. And they protested with a vengeance against a bill he proposed that dared to cut their stunningly generous entitlements.

Sarkozy was politically bloodied by what came to be known as the "Bettencourt affair" (named after L'Oreal heiress Liliane Bettencourt). To preclude his already low approval ratings from sinking still further—a feat he was mostly unable to accomplish—he appeared on prime-time television and lowered himself to reply to questions from the press. Looking drawn and subdued, Sarkozy sat on the terrace of the Élysée Palace in summer 2010 to respond to his interlocutors and insist that he had "promised to create a republic above reproach and that is what we are doing."

His appearance did not, of course, stop the scandal from continuing online—a reminder that French leaders are still being caught off guard by the tabloid sensibilities of the wired world. In addition to the Bettencourt affair, a steady stream of online videos has showed French politicians in compromising positions—some were inebriated, others were rude or even obscene.[16] Most recently, Dominique Strauss-Kahn, the Frenchman who was managing director of the International Monetary Fund, was snared in a scandal that started in a Manhattan hotel where a chambermaid accused him of attempted rape. Though the charges against Strauss-Kahn were finally dropped, he was not spared deep humiliation, which did not go unnoticed by French women. They seized the occasion to speak out as they never had before against chauvinism and sexual harassment in the workplace.

The protests against the bill that threatened those stunningly generous entitlements took place in 2010 and their scale was massive. On a single day in September, some 2 *million people* participated in strikes clear across France. Moreover, on different days there were different disruptions—in travel by train and air, in schools, in sanitation, and in access to fuel for cars and trucks. Large numbers of students and workers joined together in stoppages and street protests, and in tossing Molotov cocktails. Ultimately, the embattled and seemingly permanently unpopular Sarkozy was able to claim victory, but not before the situation got so threatening that the head of a major French polling institute warned, "We are in a situation where government and the unions are losing control, and if something serious happens, it will both weaken the unions and be a catastrophe for government."[17]

Of course the French were hardly the only Europeans in recent years to protest increased unemployment and increased austerity. In Greece, there were strikes and protests, most of which went on for months, even as the debt crisis grew critical. In Ireland they had the largest street demonstrations in years. In Spain there was a jarring vote against the ruling socialist government, a general strike, relentless protests, and a mood of malaise described as transformative.[18] And Latvia, Lithuania, and Bulgaria all experienced social and political unrest in response to the trying times. Even the British were not exempt. Described at first as being "calm" and "carrying on" in spite of budget cuts, there came a time when the worm turned. In response to government proposals to decrease spending on education and increase tuition, approximately 50,000 demonstrators gathered in London, some using force to storm the building that houses the Conservative Party, and others getting a crack at Prince Charles and his wife, Camilla, Duchess of Cornwall, by attacking their car and spattering it with paint. And in the summer of 2011 there were of course street riots in several of England's major cities, the worst by far in decades.

In spite of the fact that Germany has performed admirably in recent years, Chancellor Angela Merkel was not spared the humbling of her European counterparts. During the summer of 2010 her approval ratings were at record lows, a trend that persisted well into 2011, when more than two-thirds of Germans believed she was "undermining Germany's influence abroad."[19] Merkel was criticized for being too conciliatory (regarding a fiscal pact for the eurozone), for being divisive and directionless, and for her personal style. Said prominent publisher Josef Joffe: "Merkel doesn't inspire, she doesn't rally. She doesn't have a strategy, other than to stay in power and get things done as best as she can."[20] Additionally she and other members of the German political establishment were stunned in

2011, when the renegade Pirate Party, supposedly a fringe group focused only on Internet freedom, won nearly 9 percent of the vote in state elections in Berlin. Were the Pirates, Germans wondered, merely the punch line to a joke, or an exciting new experiment in online democracy?[21]

Finally, it should be noted that Russia was by no means the only former Soviet socialist republic in which Participants, Activists, and even Diehards made their voices heard. In 2009, tens of thousands of Georgians took to the streets to try to force their president to resign. (He did not, and the protests continued.) In 2010, 20,000 Belarusans stormed the main government building and clashed with riot police to protest electoral fraud. (One year later, a leading member of the Belarusan opposition was sentenced to five years in prison.) And in 2011, the opposition in Azerbaijan, clearly emboldened by the events in the Middle East, stepped up its opposition to the authoritarian government, in spite of the inevitable police crackdown.

Followers all over Europe have been emboldened in recent years, and leaders all over Europe have been attacked, demeaned, weakened, or rejected outright. In fact, the European Union itself is threatened as never before, undermined by political and economic strains that have emerged only in the last few years, particularly between north and south and richer nations versus poorer ones.

There are, of course, irregularities in the trajectories, and exceptions to the general rule. For example, the Scandinavian countries, blessed by both high levels of development and high levels of equity, have by and large been free of strife between those who lead and those who do not. And then there is Italy—a country whose economy lagged well behind the economies of Germany and France, and where the longtime leader was as corrupt as he was inept, but whose constituents were curiously passive, inexplicably tolerant to the inevitable end of his history of wrongdoing. I refer, of course, to Silvio Berlusconi, Italy's second-longest-serving prime minister ever (after Benito Mussolini), whose political career survived (until 2011) a series of legal charges against him, including mafia connections, tax fraud, false accounting, bribery, and paying a minor for sex. But Italy, for reasons that escape me entirely, was an exception. By and large political leaders have been much more vulnerable in the twenty-first century than they were in the twentieth.

This holds for business leaders as well. Marcel Ospel, former chairman of the United Bank of Switzerland (UBS), and Klaus Kleinfeld, former CEO of Siemens, are just two examples of European executives forced in recent years to resign. In fact, in the first decade of the twenty-first century, turnover among European CEOs was high, up to 15.3 percent. Additionally, they, like CEOs everywhere else, have demonstrably less time to prove themselves now than did those who preceded them a generation or two ago.[22]

In March 2011, the prime minister of Portugal, José Sócrates, quit because the opposition rejected his austerity package. Of course, at the time anyway, no leader could have developed an acceptable austerity package, because no leader could have crafted one that was both sufficiently stringent *and* politically acceptable. The inevitable result was that by April 2011, Portugal joined Greece and Ireland—it became the third eurozone nation to seek outside help (from the European Union, from the International Monetary Fund) as a result of its inability to resolve its financial crisis. So the Portuguese—rather like others who come to mind, say, for instance the Americans—lacked the will and skill to get their fiscal house in order. Neither government nor business, neither leaders nor followers, could save them from themselves, until finally, in June 2011, the Portuguese elected a new prime minister. Time will tell the tale of his performance, but his learning curve will in any case be steep:

Portugal's prime minister had never before held a government post—and by the end of 2011, no fewer than eight European governments had fallen in the two years previous.

Elsewhere in Asia

Here the differences can be said to outweigh the similarities. There is scant resemblance between patterns of dominance and deference in North Korea, for example, and Japan. But, in fact, Asia is like elsewhere in the world—it similarly struggles between how power, authority, and influence were exercised in the past and how they are exercised in the present. Change is evident nearly everywhere, with the two exceptions proving the general rule.

Since its inception as a communist state in 1948, North Korea has experienced no significant change in patterns of leadership and followership. After the Korean War it was sealed off from its increasingly free and prosperous neighbor, South Korea. It is primarily for this reason that North Korea is an outlier, the single country of major global consequence identifiable still as totalitarian. The leader exerts complete control while his followers are suppressed, oppressed, and repressed. Of course, how North Korea will evolve subsequent to the death, in December 2011, of its longtime ruler, Kim Jong Il, remains to be determined.

The other exception is at the other extreme—Japan. It is impossible to know how leadership and followership will be affected, if at all, over the long term by the earthquake, tsunami, and nuclear crisis of 2011. Suffice it to say here that at least until 2011, Japan, similar in this one way to North Korea, was also stuck, unable to extract itself from patterns of power, authority, and influence that in general have served its people poorly. Not only were once-great companies led in ways that left them vulnerable for the first time ever—Toyota, impervious for decades to fault, was obliged in both 2010 and 2011 to recall millions of vehicles—but Japan's government was defined by nothing so much as the "parade of prime ministers." In five years, between 2006 and 2011, Japan had no fewer than six prime ministers, one of whom lasted only eight months. For reasons relating more to its political history and culture than to anything else, Japan's problems include outmoded political parties and an ingrown leadership class. But the primary problem has been one that is by now familiar: the growing gap between what followers want and what leaders are able to deliver, particularly economically. Japanese voters want a leader "who both understands their concerns and offers the vision and courage to point a way out. What they get instead are prime ministers who worry primarily about internal party politics, consensus-building and mollifying the nation's many interest groups."[23]

Most of the other countries in Asia, ranging from Malaysia, and even more recently and strikingly to Myanmar (Burma), are different from North Korea and Japan, characterized in most cases much more by (democratic) change than by stasis.[24] The explosion of social networking in Indonesia is a good example. In 2010 Indonesia had more registered Facebook users than any country in the world, save the United States and Britain—and the largest number of Facebook and Twitter users in all of Asia. Given Indonesia's brief history with democracy, it's a small wonder the remarkably rapid expansion of online participation triggered a fierce debate between some Indonesians who see social networking as a tool for further democratizing the country's frequently corrupt political system, and other Indonesians who worry about mob rule and the loss of traditional values. While such debates matter, the issue seems mostly settled. Displeased that a statue of Barack Obama as a young man was put in a park in Jakarta, Indonesians took their complaints not to the streets but to Facebook. More than 56,000 online protests later, city leaders gave in to city citizens—they conceded that in the park only Indonesians would be honored.[25]

In India, changes in patterns of dominance and deference are particularly striking, especially those relating to its ancient caste hierarchy. At last some untouchables have broken with the past and risen in Indian society, especially in the south. As one expert put it, "The breakdown of caste hierarchy has broken the traditional links between caste and profession, and released enormous entrepreneurial energies in the south, which explains in part why during the last several decades the south took such a lead over the north."[26] Wealthy entrepreneur Chezi Ganesan is a prototype: modern in every aspect, he runs a $6 million-a-year computer chip company. But he remembers his grandfather—who stood just a rung above untouchables—being forbidden even to enter a Hindu temple or to stand near people of a higher caste. While divisions according to caste are by no means a thing of the past, they have receded nearly everywhere in India, testifying yet again to changing patterns of dominance and deference worldwide.

India is telling in another way: as is happening elsewhere in the world, when people in positions of authority fail to do what is expected of them, others step in. India has an elected prime minister, a parliament, and a large bureaucracy. But given the level of public outrage over corruption, and given the widespread perception that the nation is poorly governed, the twenty-nine-person Supreme Court has turned hyperactive, inserting itself in unprecedented ways into policy making and governance.[27] While India is not the only country where the courts are intervening, even setting public policy, it is an exceptionally vivid example of the sorts of intrusions to which leaders routinely are now subjected. Nor are Indians exempt from traditional political activism. Led after a fashion by a fasting Gandhi-like figure, Anna Hazare, tens of thousands of Indians took to the streets in the summer of 2011 to express support for his very personal campaign against the widespread corruption staining the Indian system.

Then there is India's implacable enemy, Pakistan, which is one of the most dangerous countries in the world, if only because it combines extreme political instability with a considerable nuclear arsenal. During the years 2001–2008 the Pakistani government was led by Pervez Musharraf, who had staged a military coup to seize power from a democratically elected government. However, six years later Musharraf went a step too far. In 2007 he summarily fired Pakistan's chief justice, igniting a political firestorm. In as vivid a testimony to follower power as there has been in Asia, at least in the last decade, this action triggered antigovernment, anti-Musharraf protests, led at the start by lawyers in black robes and joined later by thousands and then millions of others, hell bent on accomplishing one thing: to depose the man they considered a dictator, which in short order they did.

Since then events in Pakistan have attested to, among other things, the risks associated with leaders who are weak and followers who smell blood. Not only have Pakistan's leaders been contentious to the point of being dysfunctional, but Pakistan's followers have been too eager to escalate political disagreement to the point of political crisis. Pakistan tells a cautionary tale—of ordinary people whose reach might reasonably be said to exceed their grasp.

The "Arab Spring"—Upheavals in the Middle East

It is too early to conclude much of anything about the recent upheavals in the Middle East. While we do know it changed forever the face of regional power, we do not know yet in precisely which ways. This, though, can safely be said: the Middle East revolutions bear some resemblance to the European revolutions of two decades ago. While the events that collapsed European communism did not effect a complete transformation—several former Soviet socialist republics still are dictatorships and Putin's Russia remains authoritarian—they did forever alter Europe, economically as well as politically, something likely to happen in the Middle East as a result of the Arab Spring. And, just like the upheavals in Europe, the upheavals in the Middle East provide more evidence—if more is needed—of the trajectory from leader power to follower power.

How did this change from below come about? Earlier I discussed the Internet, the importance of its ability to create change in the Middle East, particularly in Egypt. This is not to say the Internet is a cause or an explicator of events as they unfolded in what seemed the unlikeliest of places. After all, before the world was wired hu mankind was wired, under certain circumstances, to revolt. So what happened this time around? How did it happen that "seemingly overnight," first in Tunisia and then in Egypt, there was a tectonic shift—from old order to new order, from widespread political passivity to electric political activity?[28]

Simon Sebag Montefiore has pointed out that though revolutions are set off by dramatic events, they also "reflect longstanding economic depression, not to mention rising expectations and the temptations of comparison." In the Middle East in particular, "the generational difference between their wizened pharaohs and the Twitter-obsessed youth worsened the crisis, which may yet mark the end of the ancient paradigm of the Arab rule, the wise strong sheik, el Rais, the Boss."[29] It also happens that the upheavals in the Middle East were not unforeseen altogether: there *were* hints of future ferment. For example, an article titled "Can Social Networking Turn Disaffected

Young Egyptians into a Force for Democratic Change?" appeared in the *New York Times Magazine* fully two years before the revolution in Egypt—making clear that such an upheaval was at least in the realm of the possible.[30]

Still, what was the match that lit the revolutions? To this question there is one widely agreed-upon answer: a Tunisian fruit peddler by the name of Muhammad Bouazizi. After suffering what turned out to be his last indignity at the hands of a municipal inspector in the town of Sidi Bouzid, Bouazizi purchased a can of gasoline, walked to the central square, doused himself, and struck a match. Eighteen days later he was dead of his injuries.

Almost immediately after Bouazizi's self-immolation, people poured into the streets to protest. A day later the demonstrations grew larger as well as more organized and inclusive, with opposition politicians, union members, and human rights activists standing together. In short order labor protesters joined, so that by late December, two weeks after Bouazizi had set himself on fire, Tunisia was in turmoil. President Ben Ali responded by sending in his militias, only to find organized resistance. More government attacks turned out to incite more people against the authorities, including bloggers and cell phone cameramen, many of whom had been online dissenters for years, and most of whom were only too eager first to document and then to disseminate evidence of official abuse. By early January "online, labor-union, and political-party organizers called Tunisian citizens onto the Avenue. They arrived by the hundreds of thousands, and the Tunisian Army's commanding general . . . refused to issue orders to shoot the protesters. . . . Twenty-eight days after Bouazizi's self-immolation, Ben Ali fled."[31]

The result of this outpouring of sympathy for Bouazizi was what journalist Max Rodenbeck described as "a volcano of youthful rage." No more than six weeks after Bouazizi's death, decades-long president Ben Ali of Tunisia was out, and so was Egypt's decades-long president, Hosni Mubarak. There were copycat movements across the Middle East, including in varying degrees Morocco, Jordan, Yemen, Bahrain—and Syria.[32]

Notwithstanding Syrian president Bashar al-Assad's prediction—in January 2011 he told the *Wall Street Journal* that the situation in his country was different—Syria turned out to be similarly vulnerable to popular protestations. The uprising started in March, when police arrested some schoolboys for scrawling antigovernment graffiti on walls. In response to the arrests, protests erupted and the police opened fire.[33] Thus was ignited what turned out to be an escalating cycle: followers demonstrating and leaders retaliating, violently when necessary.[34]

Clearly not every rebellion is successful—or bloodless. Iran is Exhibit A of what happens when leaders take on by any means necessary followers no longer willing to follow. In June 2009, in the wake of President Mahmoud Ahmadinejad's contested electoral victory, peaceful protests broke out across Iran—protests known to most as the Green Revolution and to some, for obvious reasons, as the Twitter Revolution. Ultimately, of course, force was used to silence the opposition, which is why Iran (along with Syria) now serves as a sober reminder of what can happen to followers when leaders strike back.

Muammar Gaddafi's response to prodemocracy rebels in Libya was similarly harsh. Before he was finally felled he was able to withstand their attacks for a surprisingly long time, even though their numbers were considerable and they had the weight behind them—including military support—of the international community. Scenes more or less the same—each a mix of resistance, chaos, and violence—were enacted throughout the Middle East, testifying yet again to this simple proposition: once revolutionists, followers, take to the streets, the ability to stop or at least to slow them depends nearly entirely on the leader's willingness to cut them off at the pass, if necessary by spilling blood.

So what can be said about events such as these, whether in Europe or in the Middle East, which change forever relations between leaders and led—whatever the interim outcome? Here are my conclusions:

First, in the twenty-first century certainly, such political upheavals are associated not only with an overthrow of the old by the new, but of the old by the young. This applies both to the old who are literally sclerotic, and to the old who have held power and authority for an unconscionably long period of time. Second, revolutions happen when the soil has been prepared by followers—by followers who feel hopeless and are furious, who feel depressed and are oppressed, and who are primed on one or another level for political action. Third, technologies do not have to be new to enable contagion. Events in the Middle East were fanned not only by new media but by old media such as Al Jazeera, the Qatar-based satellite channel whose aggressive television coverage helped spread insurgent emotions from one capital to the next. As one expert noted, "The notion that there is a common struggle across the Arab world is something Al Jazeera helped create."[35]

Fourth, the leader's initial response to rebellious followers is frequently inconsistent: he begins by giving a carrot; then, if necessary, he turns to the stick. To buy off any unrest, Saudi Arabia's King Abdullah lavished the equivalent of billions of dollars on his subjects in 2011, including pay raises, debt forgiveness, and money to buy houses and start businesses. Syrian president Assad first promised his people that he would rescind a five-decades-old draconian law that entitled the government to detain people without charges and forbade them to demonstrate unless expressly permitted to do so. Yemen's president Ali Abdullah Saleh's first response to the demonstrable anger against him was to announce concessions, including his willingness at some point to leave office (as opposed to being president for life), and a pledge his son would not succeed him. Even the kings made concessions: King Abdullah of Jordan thought it prudent to respond to weeks of antigovernment demonstrations by sending his cabinet packing; and only months after the revolutions in Tunisia and Egypt, King Mohammed VI of Morocco announced proposed constitutional changes that would reduce his own nearly absolute powers.

Finally, revolutions happen in stages—not overnight. One of the signs a political leader is likely to fall is when key associates, previously followers, begin to peel away: in Tunisia and Egypt, army officers chose the people over the potentate; in Yemen the embattled president was weakened when high-level officials deserted him in favor of those calling for his ouster; and in Libya, Gaddafi was ditched by some of his previously nearest and dearest, including Foreign Minister Moussa Koussa, who fled Tripoli for exile in London. All this is a variant of my overriding theme: the "magically spontaneous momentum" of revolution is, by definition, driven not by those up top, but by those further down, by followers who drive the action.[36]

Work in Progress

Notwithstanding persistent oppression, regular repression, and intermittent regression, the trajectory of history moves generally in a single direction: toward democratization. Still, there is no end to this story—no conclusion to bring closure or social contract etched in stone. For while the general trend is from the diminution of leader power to the expansion of follower power, long-term outcomes in specific situations remain unknown for extended periods of time. Moreover, I do not want to exaggerate or romanticize the historical trajectory. Even in strong democracies, political and economic agendas tend to be controlled by a powerful few, not by the powerless many. Still, in the twenty-first century more people are likely to have more of a say than at any other time in human history.

By necessity, the present discussion has omissions—what, for example, has been happening in Cuba and Cameroon? And there has been more emphasis on some parts of the world, such as Europe, Asia, and the Middle East, than on others. But Latin America is no more immune to change than is Africa. Student protests have crippled campuses in Puerto Rico (2011); segments of society in Chile that until recently were apathetic, including students and labor unions, have turned on corporate and political elites (2011); in Brazil environmentalists have tried for years, often as not in vain, to stop deforestation; and Cuba's communist government is loosening its grip. Similarly, notwithstanding the decades-long dictatorship of Zimbabwe's Robert Mugabe, Madagascar's president, Marc Ravalomanana, was forced to resign in 2009 after weeks of political turmoil; in South Africa in 2010, the poor protested that they were being neglected, and nationwide strikes paralyzed hospitals and schools; in 2011, in the Ivory Coast, longtime strongman president Laurent Gbagbo was finally captured after refusing for months to cede power to his democratically elected opponent; and Uganda's president of twenty-five years, Yoweri Museveni, is feeling the heat after continuing protests over the rising prices of food and fuel.

Events at the national level are being mirrored at the international level. Emerging powers are asserting themselves, playing increasingly important roles in politics and markets and in turn diminishing the importance of the United States, considered not long ago "the world's only remaining superpower." Put directly, Washington's power and influence have declined in recent years, while the power and influence of other countries, such as Brazil, Russia, India, and China (collectively known as BRIC), have been enhanced. Additionally, American presidents can no longer simply negotiate with their counterparts in other states without taking into account the passions of the street, the political preferences of ordinary people.

One could view these various events as isolated, one separate and distinct from the other. But they are not. The arc of history connects the upheavals in Europe in 1989 to the upheavals in the Middle East in 2011. Moreover, in this globalized, wired, Skyped, and smartphoned world there is a contemporaneous connection: between the protests in 2011 in Belarus and the protests in 2011 in Uganda. There is then a pattern: a link between past and present and between what happens in one place and what happens in another. "The lines of causation," wrote Timothy Garton Ash, "include the influence of individual states on their own societies, societies on their own states, states on other states, societies on other societies, states on other societies . . . and societies on other states."[37]

Which leads inevitably to this question: given that everything connects to everything else—that leaders nearly everywhere are less effective than before and that followers nearly everywhere are less supportive than before—how has the leadership industry adapted to this new and changed social contract?

Not well. This is not to say the industry has not adapted at all—as we have seen, leaders have in fact been taken down a peg or two, and followers, "team members," have stepped up a peg or two. But given the deep disappointments associated with leaders in both business and government, incremental change seems to me to be inadequate to the challenge. What we need instead is major change—a complete overhaul.

Part III

Paradigm Shift

7

Leadership Industry—
leading as mantra

Becoming a leader has become a mantra. The leadership industry has exploded in the last thirty or forty years—in part the result of the following trends: first, the historical trajectory, a shift to weakened leaders, strengthened followers, and more complicated contexts; second, an acceleration of this shift, hard on the heels of the social and political upheavals of the late 1960s and early '70s; and third, the real or perceived decline of the United States in comparison with other countries, such as Japan (in the 1970s and '80s) and, more recently, China.

The leadership industry is now global. But originally it was an American phenomenon, in keeping with Americans' can-do attitude, which, in the past anyway, was based on the assumption that any problem is solvable and that anyone can learn to do anything—including how to lead. There is also the presumption that being a leader—in sharp contrast to being a follower—is good in and of itself. It is considered a path to having power, authority, and influence, and, usually, money. And it is considered a path to personal and professional fulfillment as well as to goal achievement, in particular to creating change.

As a result of these by now conventional wisdoms, in the last few decades leader learning has become an industry in which more than $50 billion is spent annually, just on corporate training and development.[1] During the 1980s, I myself wrote and edited five books with the word *leadership* in the title. I was part of a growing trend: in the early 1980s an average of three books on leadership were published each year; by the end of the decade that number was twenty-three. By now, of course, the number of leadership books (and other related materials) is somewhere in the stratosphere (a Google search of leadership books returns more than 84 million results),[2] with most of the material based on a few simple assumptions: that leadership is a skill of some sort, which everyone everywhere should aspire to acquire; that leadership can be learned by all sorts of people, from different backgrounds, and with different experiences and areas of expertise; that notwithstanding the differences between them, leadership can be learned by large numbers of people simultaneously; that leadership can be learned quickly and easily—over a period of months or weeks or even over a weekend; that, in comparison with leaders, followers are less consequential, less valuable a commodity; that context is of secondary or even tertiary consequence; and that leaders control outcomes—which is why, the industry reasons, leaders matter more than does anyone else.

Starting Early

In spite of the rise of the follower—or, as I just suggested, *because* of it—the leader is still the star. On one level, it's no surprise: leaders always were and always will be central. But our focus has morphed into a fixation, an obsession with being a leader that, certainly in the twenty-first century, is counterfactual. It flies in the face of the obvious—that leaders now have less power, authority, and influence than they did before, and that we live in a time when other elements are determinants. Again, one could say that this is precisely why learning to lead became a growth industry—as compensation for the missing "great man." Still, to see how the world now works is to be struck by the juxtaposition between the continuing centrality of the leader in our collective consciousness and the mounting evidence that in the real world leaders matters less now, not more.

When Lawrence Summers became president of Harvard University in October 2001, he declared in his inaugural speech, "In this new century, nothing will matter more than the education of future leaders and the development of new ideas."[3] In this single sentence, Summers made three assumptions: that large numbers of men and women, roughly ages eighteen to twenty-two, can be educated to lead, that they can be educated to lead within a period of four years, and that they can be educated to lead wisely and well.

Summers's reference to "future leaders" was a departure, for the mission statement of Harvard College does not mention either leaders or leadership. Instead, Harvard College's twenty-first-century mission statement is based on Harvard College's seventeenth-century mission statement (the charter), which was to "create knowledge [and] to open the minds of students to that knowledge." So by asserting early in the twenty-first century that nothing mattered more at Harvard than the "education of future leaders," Summers was selling something new: the idea of leadership, the ideal of leadership, and the presumption that if Harvard students are to be well educated, they are to be educated to lead.

It says a lot that this theme reverberates not only at Harvard College, at the undergraduate level, but at Harvard University more generally. It turns out the words *leader* and *leadership* are in the mission statements of virtually every single one of Harvard's professional schools. (Italics that follow are mine.)

- Harvard Law School: "To educate *leaders* who contribute to the development of justice and the well being of society."

- Harvard Medical School: "To create and nurture a diverse community of the best people committed to *leadership* in alleviating suffering caused by disease."

- Harvard Divinity School: "To educate women and men for service as *leaders* in religious life and thought. . . ."

- Harvard Business School: "We educate *leaders* who make a difference in the world."

- Harvard Kennedy School: "Our mission is to train enlightened public *leaders*. . . . "

- Harvard School of Education: "To prepare *leaders* in education and to generate knowledge. . . ."

Nor is Harvard alone in this relentless attention to leadership—it permeates higher education. The mission of Dartmouth College is to educate "the most promising students" and prepare them for "a lifetime of learning and responsible leadership." One of the "mission goals" of Medgar Evers College is to "prepare students for leadership roles in a changing world." The mission statement of Bryn Mawr College encourages students "to be responsible citizens who provide . . . leadership for an increasingly interdependent world." And so on.

Among the implications of this leader-centrism is that those who are other than leaders are nothing much. Why, for example, is Harvard Law School so insistent on educating leaders? Does it no longer suffice to excel at what you do? To be a consummate professional, in this case a lawyer, who chooses, for whatever reason, to hunker down to, say, be a student of the law, rather than lead others? Why does the Harvard School of Education prefer to "prepare leaders," as opposed to, say, prepare *teachers* to shine in the classroom? And, similarly, why are American students at both the graduate and undergraduate levels pushed so hard by individuals and institutions to be leaders, when being followers, collaborators, team members, and even loners can be just as constructive?

It seems obvious to me that this apparently contagious obsession with leadership smacks more of followership—of fashion, fad, or herd—than it does of anything else. What is less obvious is the degree to which leader learning has infiltrated the curriculum. Sometimes it starts in high school. And sometimes it is leadership in name only, because the brand is hot.

Brown University's Leadership Institute is open to high school students from ninth grade through graduated seniors. Its mission is to help students develop "effective and socially responsible leadership." Georgetown University has a summer program for high school students called "Leadership and Ethics." Students attend so that they can develop their "own leadership capabilities, style, and ethical code while learning how to leverage partnerships and build coalitions." At the University of Virginia, the Sorensen Institute for Political Leadership has a High School Leaders Program that promises to "prepare future leaders for ethical and responsible citizenship and public service." And at Duke University there is a Leadership Institute, which offers high school students a two-week summer program called "Leading Strategically in the 21st Century." (In summer 2011, the cost of the program, per student, was $3,650— not including airfare, books and "some meals.")

Then there is LeadAmerica, which claims to be the nation's premier leadership organization for high school and also middle school students. It is committed to "educating and empowering young leaders," which makes it not much different from the Youth Leadership Conference, which has held annual events since 1989. The Youth Leadership Conference recruits thousands of high school students from the United States and abroad to prepare them "for college and beyond," and to enlist them in a "comprehensive leadership program designed to develop the leadership potential within each of our students."

In fact, the word *leadership* is used for all sorts of programs targeted at young people—probably to entice them by making such programs more palatable, respectable, and even desirable. For example, LEAP Programs are essentially college preparatory exercises for high school students, intended to sharpen their academic skills. But, for whatever reason, "leadership" is part of the package. Though it does not in any way reference leader learning in its promotional materials, the program is nevertheless called the "High School LEAP Leadership Program." (In 2011, one week of LEAP Leadership cost one student $2,997.) Along similar lines, a summer program (a camp really), targeted at teenage girls to build their self-esteem and boost their self-confidence is called the "Girls Leadership Institute." The Girls Leadership Institute is run by Rachel Simmons, who previously was affiliated with Oprah Winfrey's Leadership Academy for Girls in South Africa, and receives scholarship support from the Young Women's Leadership Network, an organization created to support inner-city, single-sex charter schools. *Leadership* clearly rules.

The trend extends to undergraduates everywhere, who, assuming they have any interest at all in leadership, have a range of options from which to choose. Students who themselves want to be leaders can engage in any number of undergraduate activities in addition to leadership courses—student government, sports, campus clubs and organizations—that intentionally develop leadership skills. And for those who want to learn *about* leadership, there are more traditional academic offerings, all of which can now be found on college campuses clear across the country.

Yale University has a Leadership Institute, a Women's Leadership Initiative, a Global Health Leadership Institute, a Chief Executive Leadership Institute, and an MBA on Leadership in Healthcare. Northwestern has a Center for Leadership, the University of Iowa offers a Certificate of Leadership Studies, Rice University has a Program for the Study of Leadership—I could go on . . . and on. But for all their superficial similarities, in fact the many different leadership programs conflate two quite different learning experiences. The first is leadership education for the purpose of learning how to lead—it suggests practice, a set of skills or capacities to be acquired or mastered, as in leadership development or training. The second is leadership education for the purpose of learning about leadership—it suggests theory, ideas, and information, leadership as a subject of study. This distinction, though central to the leadership industry, is nevertheless often obscured, thus similarly obscuring the fact the industry is dependent on a veneer of academic respectability. Leadership Studies—the interdisciplinary, multidisciplinary field of leadership scholarship—is a critical part of the whole, an area of intellectual endeavor essential to instruction that otherwise would seem and be superficial, even artificial.

Legitimating the Industry

Teaching *how* to lead is where the money is. Nevertheless, leadership research, leadership scholarship, is essential to the whole. It legitimates the leadership industry, which explains why as the business of teaching how to lead burgeoned, the academic investment in leadership burgeoned as well. To be clear, Leadership Studies as a field has never been and is not now entirely respectable, at least not among traditional academics, who consider it more art than science, neither rigorous nor replicable, not a suitable subject for serious study. Still, the appetite for learning to lead grew so large that leadership as an area of intellectual inquiry grew right along with it.

Of course, leadership has been a subject of study since the beginning of recorded history – think Confucius and Plato. Relatively recent pioneers included among others Max Weber in the 1920s; Mary Parker Follett and Chester Barnard in the 1930s and '40s; Philip Selznick and Peter Drucker in the 1950s and '60s; and in the 1970s and '80s James MacGregor Burns and Warren Bennis. But in the last quarter century leadership became something else altogether—a subject of study for *large numbers* of people, practitioners as well as academics from all over the world, with all sorts of different credentials and areas of expertise. Research centers proliferated, nearly all of them established in the last decade or two; the number of academic programs, including those at the doctoral and master's levels, escalated; and so did the number of academic publications on leadership, countless books and articles and refereed journals, most but by no means all published in the United States.

The academic journals include, among others, *Leadership Quarterly*, the *Journal of Leadership and Organizational Studies*, and *Leadership*, a British publication. The advanced degree programs include, among others, the University of Oklahoma's Doctorate in Organizational Leadership, the Harvard School of Education's Doctor of Education Leadership, and the Executive Master of Leadership at the University of Southern California. Most of these programs are interdisciplinary and/or multidisciplinary, and most promise the better exercise of leadership practice though the better understanding of leadership theory.

Along with the growing number of leadership professionals has been the growing number of professional organizations. For example, there is the Association of American Leadership Educators, the American Management Association (their tagline is "Leaders in Leading"), and the International Leadership Association (or ILA, of which I was cofounder). Most hold annual conferences with all sorts of leadership sessions on all sorts of leadership subjects—from "Deconstructing Leadership: The Role of Context, Personality, and Paradox" to "Ubutu: An Evolutionary Leadership Model."

In fact, Harvard University, to which I migrated in 2000 to help establish the Center for Public Leadership, has had its own share of leadership conferences in recent years, each dedicated to legitimating leadership scholarship. Several books and articles have emerged from these conferences, among them my own edited collection with Deborah Rhode, *Women and Leadership*, and another edited volume, by Nitin Nohria and Rakesh Khurana, *Handbook of Leadership Theory and Practice*.[4] The *Handbook* is an especially ambitious undertaking, providing academic perspectives on leadership theory, leadership practice, and, of course, leadership development.

I say "of course" because leadership development is without question what those within the academy as well as those without are much the most interested in—growing leaders, training leaders, teaching people how to lead. The shared assumption is that leadership development is a legitimate undertaking—that people can and do learn how to lead, from those paid to teach them, which is why so many shell out so much to buy whatever it is the leadership industry has to sell.

This makes it all the more important that academicians play their part, for as at least a few of them will admit, even if only in hushed tones, without leadership scholarship to support it, the leadership industry is hollow—an empty edifice built on shifting sand. In fact, as Nohria and Khurana themselves concede from their perch at the Harvard Business School, it will be impossible ultimately to teach leadership, at least in good conscience, unless we can "produce knowledge. . . . If society expects us to develop better knowledge about leadership and a better ability to develop leaders who will benefit society, we must meet that call or risk undermining our legitimacy."[5] What we are starting to see, then, is that for all the resources that have been poured into the leadership industry, and for all its continuing growth and remarkably wide appeal, there is at least some skepticism that it actually does what it purports to do.

Professionalizing the Industry

Given the recent rise of the leadership industry, and the recent rise of China, it was likely that at some point China would develop its own leadership programs, its own capacity to teach how to lead in keeping with its own culture. It turns out that time is now. Driving from the airport in Shanghai to the Chinese Executive Leadership Academy Pudong (CELAP), one is struck by an enormous building, utterly modern in design, that is dedicated to nothing other than learning leadership.

Like so much else in China, its leadership industry seems to be thriving—to which CELAP, big, bold, and bright red, bears witness. However, I mention China not because its leadership industry is bigger or better than that in the United States or, for that matter, anywhere else, but rather as an indicator. Leadership is not only big in China, it is government sponsored. The full weight and authority of both the Chinese government and the Chinese Communist Party are behind CELAP and everything it implies—which is that leadership training and development generally suggest not great change, but moderate change, change that can be managed and controlled, as opposed to change that gets out of hand. This is similar to, not different from, leadership training and development programs as they proliferate in the United States and elsewhere in the world.

In 2012, the publication *Leadership Excellence* had a list of the "Best in Leadership Development." It included large organizations (IBM, General Electric, Boeing, Procter & Gamble), small and mid-size organizations, universities, nonprofit programs, government programs, large consulting groups, and independent consultants, trainers, and coaches. The list was not scientific, and the rankings were not to be read as gospel. But the list did suggest the extent to which leadership development programs—programs that purport to grow leaders and/or to improve the performance of those already labeled leaders—have infiltrated virtually every sector of American society. In fact, *Leadership Excellence* is itself a signifier. Like many other publications, it has short, punchy pieces for those intent on learning to lead as expeditiously as possible. Other publications, such as the *Harvard Business Review*, are more substantial. But even they by now are composed mainly of short pieces, aimed at hyper-busy executives with short attention spans.

You want to be a leader? No problem. There are leadership development programs for nearly every possible population. The Danya Institute has a leadership development program for "emerging leaders in the addiction profession." The purpose of the Leader to Leader Institute is to "strengthen the leadership of the social sector." The U.S. Army has a document addressing "all aspects of leadership and leader development policy, doctrine, training and research."[6] And wildlife professionals are free to choose from, among others, the following: the Emerging Wildlife Conservation Leadership Program, the Great Lakes Leadership Program, the National Conservation Leadership Program, the Natural Resources

Leadership Development Program, the Nissan/World Wildlife Fund Environmental Leadership Program, and the Wildlife Society Leadership Institute.[7]

Health care is another example—a profession with a strong commitment to developing leaders. There is a National Center for Healthcare Leadership, dedicated to providing "high-quality, relevant and accountable health care management leadership." Then there is the American College of Healthcare Executives, a member of the Healthcare Leadership Alliance, which has an assessment tool that places the leader at the center of "five critical domains."[8] And, of course, nurses have their own leadership programs. A 2009 article in *Nursing Economics* describes the "nurse leader" as "a visionary for the organization and profession." But since the pressure to perform poses a challenge, nurses have their own "tool for soliciting feedback from staff regarding the effectiveness of nurse leaders."[9]

But for all the different leadership development programs targeted at all the different professionals, such programs are overwhelmingly the preserve of those in the private sector who, driven by pressure to make a profit, are particularly preoccupied with the performance of leaders and managers. In fact, the leadership industry was initially established by corporate America during the 1970s and '80s, when it was motivated to do whatever it could to forestall lower rates of profit and growing global competitiveness.

In the last thirty years, American business and American schools of business joined forces for the purpose of growing the leadership industry. Why? Because leadership development programs bestowed on corporate America benefits that included a presumably professionalized leadership cadre. And because leadership development programs bestowed on schools of business certain benefits—including money, big money.

The history of this development is told by Rakesh Khurana, who in his book *From Higher Aims to Hired Hands* traces the "social transformation of American business schools." Khurana makes a case for the connection—even symbiotic tie—between business and business schools. "One of the key factors in management's successful effort to establish its claims to the legitimacy and authority it enjoys to this day was another institution . . . the university-based business school."[10] Moreover, "the relationship between management and business schools is about how they have shaped each other as institutions. . . . [They] have reciprocally defined the ultimate ends of the corporation and shaped the means through which management seeks to achieve them."[11]

One of the consequences of this connection is leadership development, which, in addition to those earlier named, is a mainstay of the following: big business; business schools; schools of government and public administration; professional schools more generally; independent institutions and individuals dedicated to leadership training; and armies of experts, including academics, coaches, and consultants who make a living teaching leading.

To be sure, no more than about half of all U.S. companies have "mature" leadership development programs. And in 2009–10 no more than about half of all leaders and managers of U.S. companies participated in such programs. However, this means that a very large number of American companies *do* have such programs, and that a very large number of American executives *did* recently participate in such programs. Leadership development is, in short, a top priority for many of America's top corporations, with many investing more in leadership development now than they did even in the recent past.[12]

In February 2010 *Bloomberg Businessweek* published a series of articles on the "Best Companies for Leadership."[13] Organizations from around the world were "invited" to participate in the top-twenty survey, which means the results were neither objective nor based on a significant sample. Still, they suggest something about what is considered a good in-house leadership development program—good for the company and, presumably, good for the leaders and managers who enlist in the experience.

The five companies reported by *Bloomberg Businessweek* to have the best leadership development programs were General Electric, Southwest Airlines, 3M Company, Procter & Gamble, and Accenture. They had certain things in common. For example, they all put a premium on "selecting, developing, and retaining strong leaders at every level," and they all addressed a wide range of leadership challenges, from managing change to managing succession. But of the companies cited, GE is the outstanding example, for over the years it has frequently been cited as the American company with the single best leadership development program. A company website makes clear the priority: "Worldwide, we invest about $1 billion every year on training and education programs for the people of GE. The results can be measured in the increasing leadership capabilities of our own people and ultimately in the value and opportunity generated for our customers and their communities."[14]

Among American schools of business, the Wharton School at the University of Pennsylvania exemplifies this full-blown commitment to leadership development.

- The mission of Wharton's MBA program is to "develop leaders who act with a deeper understanding of themselves, their organizations, and their communities. . . ." Leadership programs are "at the heart of MBA life."

- Wharton's executive education programs similarly center on leadership development. They "delve into effective decision-making processes, power and influence, altering behaviors, recasting mind-sets, organizational change, personal negotiation styles, and investing in and managing relationships for greater impact." (Leader learning of this kind does not come cheap. In 2011, Wharton's two-week "Executive Development Program" cost $24,750—per person.)

- Then there is Wharton's Center for Leadership and Change Management. The center does have a research component, but its mission statement confirms its primary purpose is "to support the leadership development agendas of the Wharton School and the University of Pennsylvania."

The Center for Creative Leadership (CCL), headquartered in Greensboro, North Carolina, is another sort of leader learning enterprise, a freestanding institution that has been in business for more than forty years. CCL "equips clients around the world with the skills and insight to achieve more than they thought possible through creative leadership." CCL is not only long-lived, it is successful—each year some 20,000 people from all over the world participate in its programs. Which raises this question: how does it successfully compete with venerated institutions such as Wharton and the Harvard Business School, both of which carry the imprimatur of a great university? It's not as if CCL is modest in price—it is not. Senior-level executives pay $11,000 for a five-day experience called "Leadership at the Peak." A five-day leadership development program for mid- and senior-level "managers" costs $6,900. And a three-day program for "first time managers" costs $3,700.[15]

How then to explain CCL's success? The answer is the legitimating function of research. From the beginning it had a research program that justified what it did and how it sold itself. In particular, CCL has long focused on 360-degree assessment and feedback as a tool for leadership development. And, as it continues to make clear, this tool is regularly refined, and remains "a central part of CCL's research activities."[16]

Finally, a word about the literature on leadership development—that sky-high pile of primers that teach people how to lead. In general, they (like the rest of the leadership industry) are one-size-fits-all—they tell all sorts of leaders in all sorts of situations who to be and how to lead. In general they make it short—they imply that leadership can be learned in little more than the time it takes to read this. In general they make it simple—they imply that leadership can be learned by mastering the material immediately at hand. And in general they presume the power of positive thinking—that you too can learn to be a leader. Put differently, in general any focus on the follower is absent, and any mention of context is minimal.

Unanticipated Consequences

For all the large sums of money invested in the leadership industry, and for all the large amounts of time spent on teaching leadership, learning leadership, and studying leadership, the metrics are mostly missing. There is scant evidence, objective evidence, to confirm that this massive, expensive, thirty-plus-year effort has paid off. To the contrary: much more often than not, leadership development programs are evaluated according to only one, subjective measure: whether or not participants were satisfied with the experience. But, of course, even if they were, this does not prove the program had the impact it wanted or intended; in fact, the opposite might be true—it could be that the most satisfied participants were those who changed the least.

This is not to suggest that there are no leadership development programs that merit infusions of time and money, or that no institutions or individuals have benefited from the leader learning experience.[17] What I am saying is this: As a whole the leadership industry is self-satisfied, self-perpetuating, and poorly policed; that leadership programs tend to proliferate without objective assessment; that leadership as an area of intellectual inquiry remains thin; and that little original thought has been given to what leader learning in the second decade of the twenty-first century should look like. There have, of course, been curricular revisions, adjustments here and there to the existing model. But in spite of the widespread disappointment in and distrust of leaders in the society at large, and despite the seismic changes in culture and technology, there has been scant alteration to the prevailing paradigm of learning how to lead; no significant attempt to reimagine the model to extend it over a longer period of years, say, or to include significant learning in the liberal arts, or to adjust to an era in which leading is less about refining the individual and more about reimagining the collective; no obvious progress in formulating a fundamental, coherent curriculum sequenced in a demonstrably (proven) sensible and successful way; and no thought given to instructing on following, when following wisely and well is manifestly as important as leading wisely and well.

Failures of leadership are found everywhere. Polls, for instance—true, they don't necessarily mean much; maybe people are ignorant or not paying attention, or in some other way ill equipped to render judgment. Still, to ignore public opinion altogether would be foolish, especially since the growth of the leadership industry coincides directly with a drop in trust in those at the top. According to a 2011 CNN/ORC International poll, only 15 percent of Americans trust the federal government to do what is right most of the time. (In the 1950s and '60s this figure was closer to 70 percent.)

Similarly, Harvard's Center for Public Leadership found that fully 77 percent of Americans "agree" or "strongly agree" that the United States has a leadership crisis.[18] This decline in confidence has only gotten worse in recent years and it applies to varying degrees across the board—to political leaders and business leaders, to leaders in the media and sports, leaders of nonprofits, education, the military, and even to leaders of faith-based institutions, such as churches and other religious organizations. Nor is it trivial: the recent loss of faith in America's public institutions was described by researchers at Xavier University as no less than "devastating."[19]

Corporate America has taken a similar hit. Only a dismally low 7 percent of employees trust their employers, their leaders and managers; similarly, subordinates do not generally consider their superiors to be either honest or competent.[20] The recession has likely played a part in this perception, as have a rash of recent corporate scandals. Still, this lack of confidence in corporate leaders is part of a broader picture, in which those at the top are much less trusted, appreciated, and admired than previously. "America the broken," as Frank Bruni put it.[21]

Institutions have been as much an object of disdain as individuals. To take an obvious example, over the past two years Goldman Sachs's reputation has been battered and its conduct pilloried.[22] (Additionally—ironically, if you will—in 2011 it reported a quarterly loss—for the first time since 1999.) But then how to explain that Goldman made *Bloomberg Businessweek*'s list of the "Best Companies for Leadership"—despite its being so widely seen as "a symbol of everything wrong with banks, corporations, even capitalism itself"?[23] What we had, in other words, was a situation in which Goldman's leadership development program was among the most highly rated—even *after* its greed and hubris had become obvious, and even *after* its public floggings.

What does this say about our capacity to develop leaders? What does this say about the metrics we use to assess leadership development programs? And what does this say about our willingness to take to task the leadership industry for propagating what in this case could be considered a fraud? Nothing good. It says nothing good about our ability to develop leaders as ethical as they are effective, about the measures we use to evaluate leadership programs, about the industry's capacity to regulate itself and to admit publicly that something's gone wrong, or about its readiness to reinvent itself when nothing short of reinvention will suffice.

Of course, not every situation is the same. CEOs are more highly esteemed in some countries, such as India, China, and Brazil, which have enjoyed unparalleled growth in recent years, than in others, such as the United States, Britain, and Canada, which have not.[24] But still, there's a disconnect between what the leadership industry professes to be and what it actually is. Alan Murray, long associated with the *Wall Street Journal* and an old hand on these matters, wrote the following in late 2010 about General Electric, the same company that enjoys the highest possible reputation for its leadership development programs: "A decade after Jack Welch stepped down as chief executive of General Electric, he still commands remarkable respect as a management guru. The company he once led has lost its magic, the business processes he developed to battle bureaucracy have become bureaucratic themselves, and many of the 'graduates' of the Jack Welch school have since stumbled—think Bob Nardelli at Home Depot or Jim McNerney at Boeing. . . . Yet Mr. Welch and the management mythology surrounding him continue, untarnished."[25] Whether or not Murray's critique is fair, this much is true: GE's huge investment in leadership development did not, as we know by now, protect it against the market turndown. Nor did it even protect Welch's chosen successor, Jeffrey Immelt, who after a decade on the job still needed to prove that GE can "post solid growth and that its vaunted business model still makes sense."[26]

But we need neither sinking polls nor blemished reputations to confirm the obvious: in spite of our dedication to developing good leaders—from high school well into adulthood—bad leadership continues to constitute a plague. I don't necessarily mean evil leadership as in Zimbabwe, or even corrupt leadership as in Enron. I mean more ordinary and ubiquitous types of bad leadership, such as incompetent leadership, rigid, intemperate, and callous leadership.[27] We're oppressed by it, depressed by it, in spite of a leadership industry into which we have poured so much money and time, so many expectations and aspirations. Clearly one of the problems plaguing the leadership industry is its fixation on developing *good* leaders, while ignoring completely the problem of stopping or at least slowing bad leaders. Why, one might reasonably ask, is this insidious, ubiquitous issue almost never addressed? One obvious reason: there is more money to be made in teaching people how to lead than there is in teaching people how to follow—how to follow with intelligence and integrity, which sometimes entails *refusing* to follow, *refusing* to go along with leaders who are ineffective or unethical or both.

Given that the corporate sector has been the primary, presumed beneficiary of leadership development programs, and given that these programs are now a corporate staple, one might sensibly be struck by the persistence of bad leadership in American business. Where to begin, or end, the long list of names qualifying as "bad leaders"? With James Cayne, former CEO of Bear Stearns, who appeared clueless as his company collapsed? With Sam Zell, who "sucked the life" out of his media empire?[28] With Jerry Yang, who presided over the decline of Yahoo? With Tony Hayward, CEO of BP, who finally was forced out after his part in the worst environmental disaster in U.S.

history became crystal clear? With Richard Wagoner, erstwhile CEO of General Motors, who seemed to stand in the way of its recovery? Or with the aforementioned Angelo Mozilo, former CEO of Countrywide Financial who was obliged ultimately to pay $67.5 million in penalty and reparations, but who arguably never suffered punishment commensurate with his crimes? Or maybe turn to the cast of characters now held responsible for what the chairman of the Federal Reserve, Ben Bernanke, called "the worst financial crisis in global history, including the Great Depression." Cast members, who came from government as well as business, have since been accused of transgressions ranging from ineptitude to negligence to greed to the point of corruption. The crisis was, in any case, a consequence of human agency. It was not an act of God, nor an inevitable event in the tide of human affairs. Financial columnist Joe Nocera: "If only regulators had been willing to regulate; if only Wall Street had done proper due diligence on the mortgages it was securitizing; if only subprime companies had acted more honorably; if only the credit ratings agencies had said 'no' when asked to slap triple-A ratings on subprime junk. If only, if only."[29] Where, in other words, was the leadership industry when we most needed it?

Finally, I offer an assessment of academia, of where we are now in the evolution of Leadership Studies as an area of intellectual inquiry: I would say fair to middling, at best. Again, it is not as if no good work has been done, as if there are no people or programs that meet the highest standards of leadership scholarship. Rather it is that after four decades or so, progress has been, to put it politely, slow. The effect has been particularly deleterious on leadership training and development, in part because, as we will see in the next chapter, what exactly such training and development should consist of remains vague or, if you prefer, a question on which there is no appreciable agreement. One reason is that we have too many choices: too many competing experts offering too many competing pedagogies, most of which are based neither on empirical evidence nor on a well-established theoretical tradition. Moreover, we do not know which particular pedagogy best suits which particular circumstance; nor have we reached consensus on what could be considered a core leadership curriculum.

A few of the best and brightest leadership educators have themselves found fault—both with leadership scholarship and with leadership development programs. There are, in other words, embers of doubt and discontent within the leadership industry, as well as without. In 2005 Warren Bennis and James O'Toole of the Marshall School of Business, University of Southern California, argued that the "root cause of today's crisis in management education is that business schools have adopted an inappropriate—and ultimately self-defeating—model of academic excellence."[30] In 2007 Rakesh Khurana wrote that "leadership as a body of knowledge remains without either a widely accepted theoretical framework or a cumulative empirical understanding leading to a useable body of knowledge."[31] In 2010 Jeffrey Pfeffer of the Graduate School of Business, Stanford University, warned that "most books by well-known executives and most lectures and courses about leadership should be stamped CAUTION: THIS MATERIAL CAN BE HAZARDOUS TO YOUR ORGANIZATIONAL SURVIVAL."[32] And in 2010 Blair Sheppard of the Fuqua School of Business, Duke University, went so far as to acknowledge that the "financial crisis revealed fault lines that no business school is structured to address."[33] And that's not all—these many years later the most basic of all questions remains unanswered, even by those best positioned to answer it. After two days observing one of Harvard's star-studded leadership conferences, psychologist Richard Hackman asked, "What Is This Thing Called Leadership?"[34]

So what's gone wrong? Why has the leadership industry, for all its apparent successes, failed on so many levels? Why do incompetence and intemperance continue rampant? Why are ethics so elusive? Why is teaching leading full of "flaws"?[35] Why has it proved so hard to build a body of knowledge? Why are our leaders so widely disdained—and why is our trust in leaders of every stripe at a leaden low?

These are the questions to which I finally turn. I do not expect to make magic. But I do anticipate a new cut at an old problem—how to grow a good leader.

8
Leadership Complete—
leading in time

Can leadership—can learning how to lead—be taught?

The truth is, we don't know. We don't know if learning how to lead wisely and well can be taught, for the objective evidence is scant. What we do know, though, is that by and large, "the leadership industry is self-satisfied, self-perpetuating, and poorly policed," and that by and large these are trying times, in which "the leadership class" has not exactly distinguished itself.

But regardless, the long tradition that Confucius began continues to this day—the tradition of teaching leading. Confucius assumed that a man or even a boy could be taught to lead, so long as his teacher was older and wiser, a sage or a master, and so long as he, the pupil, was apt to profit from the instruction. Confucius was himself an inveterate teacher. When one of his students, a lord, asked, "What should I do in order to make the people respectful, loyal, and zealous?" Confucius replied, "Approach them with dignity and they will be respectful. Be yourself a good son and a kind father, and they will be loyal. Raise the good and train the incompetent, and they will be zealous."[1]

Plato was similarly eager to educate leaders, ideally some young, would-be philosopher-king who would one day rule wisely and well—lest there "be no end to our troubles." How, according to Plato, was this rare bird to be tutored? His education would be, in effect, lifelong, and steeped deep in a range of subjects, most not in any obvious way connected to leadership as we conceive of it, including literature, music, elementary and advanced mathematics, philosophy and metaphysics, physical exercise, and experience in both the civil service and military.

The early–twentieth-century polymath W. E. B. DuBois was another ardent advocate of leadership learning. A great intellect and activist, and the first African American to receive a doctorate from Harvard University, DuBois had a passion for developing what he called "the Best of [his] race." An essay he wrote as a young man titled "The Talented Tenth" argued for, of all things, leadership education. "The Negro race," wrote DuBois, is like all races. It is "going to be saved by its exceptional men"—that is, by its "leaders." Moreover, he insisted the talented tenth, "the best and most capable," the top tier of black American youth, be educated to lead not in vocational schools, but in the four-year liberal arts institutions for which American higher education was celebrated.

Evident even from this small sample is that learning to lead has been historically thought to take years, not months, and certainly not days; that learning to lead has been historically thought to entail expanding the mind, not contracting it by concentrating on one area of study, or one organization or institution in particular; that learning to lead has been historically thought to apply to the few, not the many; and that learning to lead has, for millennia, been considered to be critically important. In fact, precisely *because* learning to lead was considered so important, it was expected that the investment in the instruction, by student and teacher alike, would be large and long term.

Fast-forward to today, to leadership education in the twenty-first century. Recall it divides into two categories: leadership education for the purpose of learning *how* to lead, and leadership education for the purpose of learning *about* leadership. The former, on which I focus in this final chapter, is, as indicated, the most common and the most profitable, and it is largely about leadership practice, not leadership theory. To the question, then, of what should be learned when learning to lead, the industry provides four fundamental answers: first, leaders should develop certain skills, such as communication skills, negotiating skills, and decision-making skills; second, leaders should acquire awareness, in particular self-awareness; third, leaders should have experience, for example, in mobilizing and managing; and, finally, leaders should learn the difference between right and wrong—though how exactly ethics, or character, should be taught remains unclear. (We know perhaps slightly more than we used to about how to teach ethics, but the research suggests, to put it politely, "too wide a gap between professed commitments to ethical integrity and actual workplace practices." The research also confirms that agreement on what exactly constitutes good character remains elusive.)[2]

So while Confucius thought it important for leaders to be moral exemplars, and while Plato thought it important for leaders to study subjects such as math and music, and while DuBois thought it important for leaders to develop a "knowledge of life and its wider meaning," the leadership industry has homed in from the general to the particular, from the world that "underlies true life" to the real world, from the liberal arts to skill sets, from Bach to budgets. In our zeal for efficiency, and in our belief that almost anyone can and should learn to do almost anything as quickly and expeditiously as possible, we have condensed and contracted learning to lead to meet the demand for instant gratification, characteristic of the twenty-first century.

This constricted conception of leadership development explains our fixation on the leader, to the effective exclusion of nearly everyone else. And it similarly explains our definition of context, which is only the context of obvious consequence.[3] So when a company invests in a leadership program, it invests in one that is intended for and designed for that company in particular. On one level this makes good sense—why would GE want to put money into a leadership development initiative with a larger, more expansive goal in mind? Why, for that matter, would a school of education want to put money into a leadership development initiative intended for leaders in medicine? But, on another level, when GE limits leader learning to the context of GE, it limits leader learning, constricts leader learning, period. And when a school of education confines its world to the world of education, it is similarly constrained. Both sever leader learning from the larger sociopolitical context within which, necessarily, both are embedded. In consequence, we tend to train leaders writ small, rather than leaders writ large.

Given that we have nearly no reliable assessments of how effective are the various, countless leadership development programs, the discussion that follows should be read as speculative. This does not mean, however, it is without foundation. Quite the opposite: given that leaders now are weaker than before, and given that followers now are stronger, does it still make sense to develop these programs as leader-centric? Do we do leaders a favor by continuing to make "the leader attribution error"—by continuing to be myopic and omit followers from our worldview?[4] Similarly, given the contextual changes to which this book manifestly attests, does it make sense to develop leaders primarily in ways that are situation-specific? Isn't it obvious that twenty-first-century solutions to twenty-first-century problems mandate transcending the groups and organizations, the sectors and nations, of which most obviously we are members?

Searching for a Savior[5]

The leadership industry assumes that good outcomes depend on good leaders; that good leaders are good people; and that good people can be trained, or educated, or developed, to be good leaders. Thus leadership development is the equivalent of individual development. Put another way, whereas ideally the leadership industry is dedicated to searching for a savior, a single individual who is the apotheosis of the "great man" or great woman, more practically it is dedicated to training a leadership cadre, a cadre of consummate professionals, who can and will take charge.

In recent decades, several leadership experts developed ways of teaching how to lead that had particular resonance. Examples from my own institution, Harvard University, include John Kotter (Business School), who distinguished between management and leadership and focused on the second over the first.[6] And Ronald Heifetz (Kennedy School), who in a book titled *Leadership Without Easy Answers* developed the idea that leadership is "adaptive work" that requires "mobilizing people to tackle tough challenges."[7] And Bill George (Business School), whose ideas on "authentic leadership," leadership rife with "purpose, meaning, and values," had considerable impact.

Additionally, there are examples such as Robert Greenleaf, who was an executive with AT &T and whose conception of "servant leadership" has over the years become part of the leadership lexicon.[8] Greenleaf's ideas tap into the temper of the times, in which people are sick and tired of ego-driven leaders and long instead for servant leaders, who are self-effacing rather than self-interested, other-directed rather than self-directed. Greenleaf's servant leader is reminiscent of another type of leader who similarly captured our collective interest: James MacGregor Burns's transformational leader. Burns writes that "transforming leadership occurs when one or more persons engage with others in such a way that leaders and followers raise one another to high levels of motivation and morality."[9] Both the servant leader and the transformational leader have merit that is intrinsic—recall the social contract—and both include followers in the process of creating change.

In addition to the above are scores of other leadership experts, a number of whom (including me) can be found expounding on the subject of teaching leadership in a recent volume edited by Scott Snook, Nitin Nohria, and Rakesh Khurana titled *The Handbook for Teaching Leadership*. Though the editors acknowledge in their introduction that the "current state of leadership education lacks the intellectual rigor and institutional structure required to advance the field beyond its present and precariously nascent state," and though they enumerate some serious (one might argue fatal) flaws, they nevertheless present, in some thirty subsequent chapters, a comprehensive (if not all-inclusive) picture of prominent pedagogies.[10] The various ways to teach leadership are exciting, or intimidating, or simply confusing—take your pick. They range from courses that focus on content (what students need to know) to courses that focus on process (how change happens), to courses that focus on structure (conditions under which change takes place).

To say that each of the pedagogies is different from the others is to say the obvious; after all, that's the point of the exercise. What is less obvious is how they are similar, how nearly every one is a variation on several recurring themes.

- Most of the pedagogies are leader-centric. This seems a given— after all, this is a handbook for teaching *leadership*. But as I have argued all along implicitly or explicitly, the model, the fundamental model based on the leader at the center, is wrong. Leader-centrism no longer explains, if it ever did, the way the world works.

- Most of the pedagogies are oblivious to the fact that follow- ers matter. Why? First, because most of the pedagogies were developed in schools of business, where followers matter even less than they do in schools of government; second, because, as indicated, there is a lot of money to be made in develop- ing leaders, and not a lot of money to be made in developing followers; and third, most important, because followers are still considered inconsequential. But as we we know full well by now, followers, matter. They cannot then, must not then, be excluded from the learning process.

- Most of the pedagogies are concerned only with maximizing good leadership, as opposed to minimizing bad leadership, an imbalance that can be explained only if you follow the money. Again, there is good money to be made teaching how to be a good leader; there is no money to be made teaching how to stop or slow a bad one. Still, a rough equivalent can be drawn to teaching medical students everything they should know about maintaining good health while teaching them nothing they should know about eliminating bad health—about how to remedy whatever it is that ails us. The first is important but so, equally, is the second.

- Most of the pedagogies assume that good leadership can be taught, with little or no objective evidence to support the as- sumption. To be sure, the idea that leadership can be taught has been around since time immemorial. But one is struck by the fact that in the twenty-first century the leadership industry

is still so bereft of empirical evidence to confirm or discon-
firm whatever the pedagogical assumptions. This lack of hard
evidence leaves unanswered the question of how exactly leader
teachers should decide what exactly to teach leader learners.

- Most of the pedagogies have a constrained rather than expansive conception of context. To be sure, references to context
are made in several places throughout *The Handbook for Teaching Leadership*. But in part because of the way leader learning
is structured—invariably the instruction is relatively short
in duration and usually the presumption is one size fits all—
context is usually treated hastily and superficially rather than
over time and in depth.

The problem of pedagogy has been exacerbated, especially in
the last few years, by what in my view is an evolution with insidious
implications: from the leader as a generalist, with an interest in the
common good, to the leader as a specialist, a consummate professional trained for a particular professional purpose. This evolution
has been hastened by the shift from the development of corporate
leaders in schools of business to the development of corporate leaders in-house, where learning is tailored to meet in-house, specific,
corporate needs.[11] The most highly rated of these leadership programs are significant in size and scope, and they are expensive.
What they are not, however, are departures from the norm. That
is, like so many other leadership development programs, they are
leader-centric and, mostly, situation-specific, in this case specific
to the needs of the particular firm. Here is a look at three, beginning with Goldman Sachs.

Goldman's leadership programs provide opportunities for leadership development at every level, from entry-level employees to
experienced managing directors. Intended to sustain "the firm's
leading position in the world's financial markets," Goldman's lead-

ership initiative originated in a 1999 letter to shareholders, written by none other than then-CEO, Henry Paulson. Paulson made clear his position: that Goldman should and would devote "more time and attention to the formal training and development of leaders, particularly senior leaders."

In the past, Goldman's managers had learned to lead by apprenticeship, by working closely with their superiors. But as the leadership industry grew, and provided models for Goldman to emulate, it seemed to Paulson and some of his colleagues that the firm should commit to leadership development, as Jack Welch had done at GE. So Goldman established a "Leadership Development Advisory Committee," which concluded, first, that the "people thing" was of paramount importance; second, that the firm should take a more systematic approach to leadership development; third, that it should focus on "high potential leadership"; and finally, that it should depart from the traditional classroom model to focus on "real work," on real projects with which Goldman was directly involved.[12]

Within a few years, Goldman had made a significant investment in leadership development. For example, it launched a Global Leaders Program that recruited second-year students from "leading" colleges and universities to "empower the next generation of leaders with the skills and networks they will need to thrive in the twenty-first century." More significant was Goldman's Pine Street initiative. Established in 2001, the purpose of Pine Street was to "develop world-class leadership and management skills for the firm's Partners and Managing Directors, as well as key external clients." Pine Street featured leaders teaching leaders, business-relevant applications, and intentional investing in individuals considered the future of Goldman Sachs.

During the next decade, Pine Street, and particularly its Leadership Acceleration Initiative, became integral to Goldman's corporate culture.[13] It provided top-flight Goldman executives with an intensive six-month experience, including classroom activities, outside assignments, coaching, seminars, skills training, and action learning.[14] But that's only part of Goldman's leadership program. There is also Goldman Sachs University, which builds "critical managerial skills at the individual level, improves team performance at the group level, and offers interventions to improve individual and team effectiveness"; and the Experienced Leader program, which was developed in 2005 to "enhance participants' understanding of their dual roles as leaders of people and motivators of teams."[15]

Obviously, for more than a decade Goldman's corporate culture has been dedicated to leader learning, to developing its in-house leaders. In fact, despite the severity of the financial crisis and denigration of Goldman's reputation, CEO Lloyd Blankfein remained committed to what he (along with Paulson, his immediate predecessor) had crafted. When asked by a reporter from the *New York Times* whether the "last couple of years [had] changed, even in a small way, the kind of people you hire," Blankfein replied, "I don't think so."[16]

There is a chapter in *The Handbook for Teaching Leadership* on Goldman's leadership programs that addresses the "limitations" of its approach, citing issues such as scalability and transparency. Still, the larger question remains unasked. Given its enormous investment in leadership development, how did Goldman get into so much trouble? (In 2011, its stock price declined precipitously.) To which I would reply, how could it not? How, given its limited purpose, maximizing profit, can any in-house leadership program provide its participants with the broadly based, objectively grounded learning experience that is required for leadership writ large, as opposed to leadership writ small?

As we have seen, GE is often cited as having the best corporate leadership development program—best so far as its own corporate interests are concerned. Again, it features a range of different initiatives: GE's Entry-Level Leadership Program offers recent college graduates "prized development opportunities that combine real-world experience with classroom study"; GE's Experienced Leadership Program matches "high-potential talent" with "some of the top innovators in their fields"; and GE's Experienced Commercial Leadership Program, intended for recent MBAs, requires a two-year commitment consisting of three high-impact eight-month assignments and six weeks of global training. Finally, there is the jewel in the crown: the John F. Welch Leadership Development Center—a fifty-three-acre campus in Crotonville, New York, said to be at the forefront of "cutting-edge thinking in organizational development, leadership, innovation and change."[17]

The Crotonville experience is "something of a pilgrimage," which includes courses in leadership and innovation, courses for new managers, and skills courses such as hiring and team-building. Based on the proposition that GE should have leaders at all levels, Crotonville constitutes the capstone of a leader learning experience that ideally begins at the level of the undergraduate and continues on from there.

Of course, just as Goldman's leadership initiative is open to question—is good leadership tantamount only to good earnings and, if yes, should it be?—so is GE's. On the one hand are several academics whose findings suggest that GE is "a unique developer of CEO talent"—that GE develops more leaders than other companies and more, in fact, than GE itself can usefully absorb.[18] On the other hand is GE's performance, which was lambasted in recent years for everything from being an "investor disaster" to favoring ventures in China to having a business model that is "broken" and a CEO, the aforementioned Jeffrey Immelt, who is unable to fix it.[19] Not that the slings and arrows stopped Immelt from selling GE generally and leadership specifically. In a speech he delivered at the U.S. Military Academy at West Point in 2009, Immelt declared, "Leadership is the essence of what you will do when you graduate."[20]

We turn finally to IBM, one of America's blue-chip companies, which was in the business of leadership development before leadership development became the rage. Even under fabled CEO Thomas Watson Jr., who led IBM from 1952 to 1971, the company was known for providing its people with experiences in lifelong learning, including, of course, learning how to lead. So, during the heyday of the leadership industry, IBM simply expanded a program it had launched decades earlier. This explains at least in part why by 2009 IBM was spending nearly $700 million annually on leadership skills building alone, and it accounts at least in part for why it was ranked number one that same year among *Fortune*'s "Top Companies for Leaders," the only technology company to make the top twenty.[21]

The IBM Institute for Business Value provides "leading edge thought leadership and practical insights for business executives." To conduct its applied research it retains a roster of more than fifty consultants, who write reports such as "Integrated Talent Management" and "Global CEO Study."[22] The latter, based on interviews with 1,100 leaders from forty countries, addressed the question of how leaders can equip employees with the expertise and experience they need in today's global environment. It concluded that twenty-first-century leaders require a new set of leadership competencies, which put a premium on communicating and mutual understating.[23]

While IBM's investment in leadership is everywhere in evidence, and while the company continues to support research on "leading edge thought leadership," perhaps nothing so vividly depicts IBM's commitment to leadership at the global level as its Corporate Service Corps (CSC).[24] The CSC was launched in 2008 to prepare its leaders and managers to address this question: "How does a company develop leaders who have the skills needed for a globally integrated smarter planet?" The CSC exposes "high performance IBM employees to the twenty-first-century context for doing business," combining leadership training with service to communities and organizations, particularly in developing countries. By 2011 IBM was able to announce that it was deploying, in this case to Ghana, its one hundredth CSC team and its one thousandth CSC employee.

The CSC should not be mistaken for the Peace Corps, with which it has sometimes been compared. (Among other reasons, IBM sends its people abroad for only one month.) To the contrary, though CSC is intended also to benefit emerging countries, it is first and foremost a corporate leadership development program, intended to deliver for IBM in particular.[25] Precisely because it is rather an odd duck, because the purpose of CSC is "not so much to teach specific business skills as it is to instill the qualities individuals require to become leaders in a globally integrated business," IBM actually had the program evaluated. The bottom line: there is nothing about the CSC that is particularly innovative. Nevertheless, it does bundle common corporate practices, such as overseas postings for the purpose of leadership development, into a new and effective package.[26] And it does serve as a model. Companies such as Novartis, FedEx, and Dow Corning are developing similar such programs, and the U.S. Agency for International Development recently signed a memorandum of understanding with IBM to create the Alliance for International Corporate Volunteerism, based on the CSC. In fact, Sam Palmisano, who resigned as CEO of IBM in 2011, is credited with leadership generally, and strong leadership programs particularly.

Obviously companies such as Goldman, GE, and IBM take leadership development seriously—very seriously. However, just as obviously they all fixate on leaders (and managers) to the effective exclusion of nearly everyone else, and they fixate on themselves, that is, on their companies, to the effective exclusion of near everything else. (Even IBM's CSC program is not really an exception to this general rule.) This leader-centrism combined with this situational specificity permeates the private sector particularly, and it permeates the leadership industry more generally, even in the twenty-first century.

Searching for the Truth

If I were to develop a complete leadership curriculum, a curriculum to develop leaders for the common good, I would reimagine, reinvent the entire enterprise. At a minimum, here is the list of the assumptions—none of which will by now surprise—I would question. They underpin the leadership industry, but in my view, as they stand, they do the industry a disservice. Moreover, they add to, rather than subtract from, America's leadership crisis.

- *That notwithstanding the ostensibly flattened hierarchy, leaders are where the action is.* In his column in the *New York Times* titled "Corner Office," Adam Bryant asks CEOs the sorts of questions on which we fixate: What is your approach to leadership? What are the important leadership lessons you've learned? How has your leadership style changed? How would you sum up your leadership philosophy? And what were some early leadership lessons for you? General David Petraeus exemplifies the approach. Not only has he himself been depicted as a hero-leader, who saved the United States from recent military misadventure, he himself claims that what the armed services really need are "pentathlete" leaders—leaders so exceptional, so singular, they befit a position more intellectually challenging, physically exhausting, and politically bruising than ever.[27]

- *That the wider world (larger context) matters only insofar as it pertains to the narrower one (smaller context).* Such situational specificity leads to what I have elsewhere described, derogatorily, as "insular" leadership—leadership where the leader minimizes or disregards "the other"—that is, those outside the group or organization for which the leader is directly responsible.[28] This explains why, for example, a business like Goldman Sachs has generally been so fabulously profitable while at the same time "perverting the market instead of correcting it."[29] It similarly explains why leaders are so bad at crossing the divide, at exercising intergroup leadership as opposed only to in-group leadership.[30] And finally it explains our tendency to "bounded awareness," to ethical gaps that are the result of excluding information from the decision-making process.[31]

- *That so far as the private sector is concerned one criterion is paramount—financial performance.* An article in *Harvard Business Review* titled "The Best Performing CEOs in the World" frankly reflected the prevailing sentiment: it ranked corporate leaders *only* on the basis of stock returns. While the authors conceded that "shareholder return is not the only measure of performance," they went on to add, correctly, of course, that it is "the fundamental scorecard for CEOs of public companies."[32] This is no way to run a business—that is, it is no way to run the leadership industry.

- *That leadership is a profession for which a professional education is optimal.* While some would argue the assertion, it remains the rationale for almost all leadership development programs. Consider the case of the Harvard Business School, and its dean beginning in 2010, Nitin Nohria. Soon after becoming dean, Nohria declared, "If we are interested in educating leaders whom others declare to be leaders, we have to recognize that people only call someone a leader if they feel confident about his or her competence and character."[33] But it turns out the

Harvard Business School has had a problem—two problems, in fact. The first is specific: its own reputation for having stellar students has been, fairly or unfairly, tarnished by the financial crisis. The second is more general: business schools, virtually all business schools, are increasingly vulnerable to the charge that they are less good than they should be at developing leaders as ethical as they are effective. So Nohria is trying to fix what's broke: to professionalize, systematize, legitimize, and also globalize the education of corporate leaders. Of course whether this can be done as he would wish it—within the essentially conventional confines of an essentially conventional business school curriculum—remains an open question.

- *That leadership can be taught to virtually anyone and everyone and that leadership can be taught, simultaneously, to large numbers of different people in different situations.* Accenture, one of America's preeminent management consulting companies, believes that "leadership does not require formal authority or personal charisma, that every person has the capacity to effectively lead with integrity, and that this capacity can be developed over time through disciplined practice."[34] But do we know this is so? Can we prove this is true? Does it even make sense to make the claim that "every person has the capacity to effectively lead with integrity"? Does it even make sense to teach so many different people in so many different situations at the same time and in the same way? Would Plato agree; would Plato approve?

- *That leadership can be learned quickly and easily, as opposed to slowly and carefully.* Is it possible that the ancients, the great leader-teachers of the distant past, such as Confucius, and Aristotle, and Plato, and, for that matter, Machiavelli, were simply wrong when they proselytized that leader learning was a process long and hard and broadly based rather than narrowly focused?

- *That leadership should be taught in silos—for example in different professional schools for different professional audiences.* In the past decade, Fortune 100 companies have killed 2.9 million jobs in America, while adding 2.4 million abroad.[35] So how does it make sense for government to try on its own to solve the problem of unemployment—as in President Obama's 2011 proposal for an American Jobs Act? Why have our political leaders not collaborated much more closely and consistently with our corporate leaders on a problem as obviously trans-sector as this one? Because they are not trained or educated or even socialized, except maybe at the margins, to do so.

- *That leadership can be codified and summarized and packaged.* According to Harvard University's Center for Public Leadership (of which I was in the past both executive director and research director), there are "seven essential competencies for public leadership." (They are: personal, interpersonal, organizational, systemic, catalytic, contextual, and theoretical.) According to Linda Hill and Kent Lineback, there are "3 imperatives for becoming a great leader." (They are: managing yourself, managing your network, and managing your team.)[36] According to Jeffrey Gandz and his colleagues, good leaders do five things. (They are: analyze the environment, formulate winning strategies, execute "brilliantly," evaluate outcomes, and build for the future.)[37] And according to Jim Kouzes and James Posner there are five key leadership practices. (They are: modeling the way, inspiring a shared vision, challenging the process, enabling others to act, and engaging the heart.)[38] Can leadership possibly be so simple, so neat, so perennially positive an undertaking?

- *That the only thing worth learning is that which obviously is applicable—because that which is not obviously applicable is not relevant.* The platonic ideal—the ideal in which leader learning is equated with subjects such as, among others, music and math—is out the window. By assuming that leadership is a profession, leader learners are perforce educated as professionals, that is, narrowly rather than broadly. But what if leadership is not a profession? What if becoming a leader is not like becoming a doctor or a teacher? What if the kind of learning it entails is as much art as science, requiring immersion in, among other things, the liberal arts—subjects such as history, philosophy, and literature, and for that matter music and art?

- *That leadership is all-important and followership is unimportant.* Anyone who knows my work even some, anyone who has done so much as glanced at this book knows by now I think this ridiculous. Followers matter; they have always mattered and they matter more now than before. To exclude followership from the leadership curriculum is theoretically indefensible and practically irresponsible. Just as we encourage learning how to lead, we should encourage learning how to follow—how to engage; how to collaborate and compromise; how to serve and support good leaders; how to challenge and even take on bad leaders; how to speak truth to power. Whatever happened to the idea of educating not for leadership—but for *civics*?

- *That good leadership is all-important and bad leadership is unimportant.* The problem with this skewed view is really very simple: never in a million years will we figure out how to stop or at least slow bad leadership if we continue constantly, chronically, willfully to ignore it. The press doesn't ignore it. Nor does the public. So ask yourself, why does the leadership industry? Why does the industry fail by and large to address even these basic questions: how to preclude bad leadership from happening in the first place; what to do if and when it starts to take root; and how to assure the punishment fits the crime?

- *That patterns of dominance and deference change only slightly over time and, at that, only over long periods of time.* The idea that leadership and followership are fundamentally different from what they were even a decade ago is generally unexamined, and the materials that are used, the books, for example, are frequently dated. This is not to say there is no appreciation of change at all—to the contrary. Leaders are constantly being cautioned to beware the brave new world of social media. But the deeper implications of this change, particularly as they relate to relations between leaders on the one hand and followers on the other, remain largely unexplored.[39]

The leadership industry is less than forty years old. But even in this short span it has convinced countless clients and consumers to buy what it has to sell. Why? Because leadership taps into our deepest, most primitive human impulses. We hunger ourselves to have power, authority, and influence and, simultaneously, we long ourselves to be led wisely and well.

Absent a Magic Bullet

I recommend the buyer beware—of the leadership industry. I do not suggest that there are no great leaders, or that learning to lead is impossible, or that the instruction is an illusion. What I am suggesting is that we look at the industry more critically, improve our assessment of what is being accessed, expand our conception of what constitutes a leadership curriculum, and broaden our understanding of how change is created.

In a perfect world we would develop an overarching leadership theory with an overarching application to leadership practice. But in this imperfect world we have yet completely to understand historical causation, and to entirely explain human motivation. We have yet collaboratively to develop a core leadership curriculum, to objectively, rigorously measure the efficacy of what we do, and to fit leader learning to the twenty-first century. We do not even know how, or when, at which point in the life span, to teach that most fundamental of all leadership lessons: doing right, not wrong.

What we do know, though, is this: that in the second decade of the twenty-first century political leadership is different from before—and more difficult to exercise. Tyrannical leaders are by and large doomed, while democratic leaders are by and large constrained to the point of being impaired. They are impaired by ideologies that underpin democracy; by structural strings that include institutional checks and balances; by technologies that enable and expand dissemination of information and freedom of expression; and by followers feeling more important and entitled, and being more emboldened. Four decades ago the literacy rate among women in Saudi Arabia was 5 percent. Today 60 percent of college students in the kingdom are women—and in 2011 a growing group of Saudi women demanded, of all things, in addition to the right to vote, the right to drive. Four decades ago Mao Zedong still ruled China with an iron fist. In 2011 some 26 million messages posted on Weibos—a Twitter-like microblog platform—took on Chinese authorities by flat-out contradicting the official version of what happened when a train wrecked, killing and injuring more than two hundred persons.

Nor are corporate leaders immune from the same, general pressures. Notwithstanding the leader-centrism that permeates the leadership industry, those up high are weaker than they were, and the contexts within which they operate are more complex. Corporations are transparent to the point of being "naked," while voices from both inside the company and without are harsher and louder and carry much further.[40] New media and old opine 24/7, and as CEOs from Rupert Murdoch to Reed Hastings would be the first to testify, whenever there is a crisis, no organization, no company, can begin the "long haul back to public respectability . . . without the person at the top either resigning—or accepting blame and explaining what went wrong."[41] Additionally, corporate leaders are obliged in the present as they were not in the past to be mindful of "externalities"—of the effect they (their companies) have on the world around them, for example on the environment.

Again, to some degree, changes such as these are the product of generational differences. In 2010, nearly 90 percent of the world's top two hundred firms were led by baby boomers.[42] But right behind them are the "Net Geners," Generation Y'ers who were born between roughly 1980 and 2000 and who differ significantly from their immediate predecessors.[43] "The Net Geners have grown up with computers; they are brimming with self-confidence; and they have been encouraged to challenge received wisdom. . . . Not all of this makes them easy to manage."[44] The leadership literature is, in fact, replete with similar such cyber-cautions, such as this one, about a CEO whose "semiprivate comments would enter a very public realm—the blogosphere—unleashing a storm of controversy around him and his company."[45] Or this one, about "a world where one angry tweet can torpedo a brand."[46]

Finally, there are pressures on corporate leaders and managers to lead and manage more equitably, more democratically, than did their predecessors. Some of this is simply cultural: we know by now that twenty-first-century conceptions of good leadership imply cooperating and collaborating as opposed to commanding and controlling. But there is an additional, functional reason for sharing power and influence—it's good for business. If you lead a "co-creative enterprise," an enterprise that cares about stakeholders including employees, suppliers, distributors, and regulators, your reward will be, in addition to feeling warm and fuzzy, higher profits.[47] In fact, first on a list of "top five recommendations" on how to restore confidence in business was developing "a new stakeholder approach." CEOs were advised to talk "less about benefits to shareholders and short-term profits and instead focus on customer needs, investment in workers and sustainability (from ecology to education)."[48] To return to language that I have used here, corporate leaders are advised to adhere to the social contract by being as ethical as they are effective, by taking into account, in addition to self-interest, the public interest.

It's enough to give anyone a headache—that's how complex the context, how daunting the problems.

They are international: "The burning of fossil fuels has raised atmospheric levels of heat-trapping carbon dioxide by 40 percent above what they were before the Industrial Revolution. The added heat in the atmosphere retains more moisture, ratchets up the energy in the system, and incites more violent and extreme weather. . . . [Moreover] tropical diseases such as malaria, dengue fever, and yellow fever [will] reach temperate regions. . . ."[49]

They are regional: "The biggest economic problem facing Egypt, Tunisia, and many other Arab countries . . . is posed by demography. During the past thirty years, infant mortality in the region has fallen by more than half. Fertility rates have also dropped, but not as quickly. The result is a rapidly expanding population, with vast numbers of young people. In Egypt, the median age is twenty-four. In Yemen, it is eighteen."[50]

And they are national: "The core issue [facing the United States] is the accumulation of deeper structural problems that this recession has exposed—unsustainable levels of debt, an inability to generate middle-class incomes, a dysfunctional political system, the steady growth of special-interest sinecures and the gradual loss of national vitality. The number of business start-ups per capita has been falling steadily for the past three decades . . . The American working class . . . is being decimated, economically and socially."[51]

No wonder Americans are depressed—often down and sometimes out. Three out of four believe the economy is stagnant or getting worse. One in three is uneasy about getting married, starting
a family, or being able to buy a home. Trust in institutions is at historic lows. Large majorities think the country is on the wrong track.
And large pluralities believe their children will have fewer opportunities than they did.[52]

And no wonder the leadership industry seems so puny in comparison, so meager against the magnitude of the challenge, so
utterly unable on the whole to inspire whatever the requisite imagi-
native interventions and creative collaborations.[53] The problems
seem intractable, or at least overwhelming—more than Goldman,
GE, or IBM can begin to take on, more than the typical leadership
curriculum has any appetite for, more than the leadership industry is generally willing to concede or even entertain. The fact is,
the world is changing faster than before and more than before.
Decades-old governments and businesses disappear overnight.
New ones—new governments, new businesses—spring up, seemingly out of nowhere. Politics is roiling, innovation is accelerating,
competition is intensifying, and globalization is expanding. The
world of the second decade of the twenty-first century is networked
and interdependent and transnational—with leaders weaker and
followers stronger, or at least less pliable.

So we need to think big—far bigger and more expansively than
the leadership industry has up until now. We need to consider new
forms of engagement to preclude government from promising more
than it can deliver, and business from ignoring issues as insidious
as unemployment and gross income inequity. We need to develop a
different model for national collaboration to forestall dysfunction,
the hyperpartisanship that prevents us from even beginning to address the most intractable of our collective problems. And finally we

need to develop a higher level of contextual intelligence to practice as well as preach international cooperation—*inter*group leadership and followership, as well as *intra*group leadership and followership. We need to think of leadership as a creative act—for which leaders and followers *both* are educated, for which leaders and followers *both* are prepared over a lifetime of learning.

This book is about changing patterns of dominance and deference—and about how and why the leadership industry falls short of what some of us had wanted and intended. It is not about simple solutions. Historian David Greenberg has pointed out that almost anyone who writes a book aspiring to analyze a social or political problem provides an "obligatory prescription." But he further points out that nearly always such prescriptions are utopian, pedestrian, or out of tune with the rest of the book. When it comes to social criticism, no one "has an exit strategy."[54]

To this general rule, I am an exception—I am refraining from an "obligatory prescription." What I will say, though, is this: leadership is in danger of becoming obsolete. Not leaders—there will always be leaders—but leadership as being more consequential than followership, leadership as learning we should pay to acquire, leadership as anything better than business as usual, leadership as a solution to whatever our problems, and leadership as an agreement of which merit is a component. To preclude this possibility—the possibility of its own obsolescence—the leadership industry must, at a minimum, make four changes. It must end the leader-centrism that constricts the conversation. It must transcend the situational specifics that make it so myopic. It must subject itself to critical analysis. And it must reflect the object of its affection—change with the changing times.

Notes

Introduction: Twenty-First-Century Leadership and Followership

1. Toni Bentley, " 'Vindication': Mary Wollstonecraft's Sense and Sensibility," *New York Times*, May 29, 2005.
2. "Declaration of Sentiments," Seneca Falls, NY, 1848.
3. The greatest impact of *The Feminine Mystique* was on white, middle-class women, to whom it particularly applied. In 1960 only 27 percent of such women held jobs outside the home, compared to 64 percent of their black counterparts. See Stephanie Coontz, *A Strange Stirring* (New York: Basic Books, 2011).
4. The exception to this general rule is money. Men still earn more than do women, even for the same work, and they generally accumulate more, much more, over their lifetimes. Put another way, mothers are more likely to be poor than fathers. Still, see Hanna Rosin, "The End of Men," *The Atlantic*, July 2010.
5. Stephanie Coontz, *Marriage, A History* (New York: Viking, 2005), http://www .stephaniecoontz.com/books/marriage/chapter1.htm; see also, Kate Bolick, "All the Single Ladies," *The Atlantic*, November 2011. For an argument about a different sort of change over time, the decline of violence, see Steven Pinker, *The Better Angels of Our Nature: Why Violence Has Declined* (New York: Viking, 2011).

6. John Deutsch, "An Assignment for Joe Nye," unpublished paper, May 17, 2011.

7. David Brooks, "Who Is James Johnson?," *New York Times*, June 17, 2011, p. A35.

8. For more on followers, see Barbara Kellerman, *Followership: How Followers Are Creating Change and Changing Leaders* (Boston: Harvard Business School Press, 2008).

9. Kellerman, *Followership*, passim.

10. On the similarities between leadership in business and government, see Barbara Kellerman, *Reinventing Leadership: Making the Connection Between Politics and Business* (Albany: State University of New York Press, 1999).

11. The figures are from Deborah L. Rhode and Amanda K. Packel, *Leadership: Law, Policy, and Management* (New York: Wolters Kluwer, 2011), p. 6.

Chapter 1: Historical Trajectory—*lessening power*

1. Joseph Campbell, *The Hero with a Thousand Faces* (Princeton, NJ: Princeton University Press, 1973), p. 4

2. Sigmund Freud, "Group Psychology and the Analysis of the Ego" in Barbara Kellerman, *Leadership: Essential Selections on Power, Authority, and Influence* (New York: McGraw-Hill, 2010), p. 83.

3. Campbell, *The Hero with a Thousand Faces*, p. 30.

4. For a recent discussion on our need for heroes, see William Deresiewicz, "An Empty Regard," *New York Times*, August 21, 2011.

5. Thomas Carlyle, "On Heroes, Hero-Worship, and the Heroic in History" in Kellerman, *Leadership*, p. 57.

6. Hayley Tsukayama and Liz Lucas, "Thousands Cheer Obama at Rally for Change," *Columbia Missourian*, October 30, 2008.

7. Campbell, *The Hero with a Thousand Faces*, p. 15.

8. Kurt Luedecke quoted in Barbara Kellerman, *Followership: How Followers Are Creating Change and Changing Leaders* (Boston: Harvard Business Press, 2008), p. 99.

9. Quoted in Kellerman, *Followership*, p. 54. Freud's last book is titled, *Moses and Monotheism*. Though Freud was writing about Moses, it is widely agreed that he raised a question such as this one in particular response to the rise of Hitler.

10. Quoted in Kellerman, *Leadership*, p. 13.

11. Quoted in Kellerman, *Leadership*, p. 17.

12. Quoted in Kellerman, *Leadership*, p. 35.

13. Quoted in Kellerman, *Leadership*, p. 49.

14. Steve Pincus, *1688: The First Modern Revolution* (New Haven, CT: Yale University Press, 2009), p. 475.

15. Kellerman in *Leadership*, p. 49.

16. Quoted in Kellerman, *Leadership*, p. 126.

17. T. H. Breen, *American Insurgents, American Patriots: The Revolution of the People* (New York: Hill & Wang, 2010) p. 16.

18. My complete typology of followers is in *Followership*, passim.

19. Quoted in Barbara Kellerman, *The Political Presidency: Practice of Leadership* (New York: Oxford University Press, 1984), p. 4.

20. Samuel P. Huntington, *American Politics: The Promise of Disharmony* (Cambridge, MA: Harvard University Press, 1981), p. 33.

21. Henry David Thoreau, "Resistance to Civil Government."

22. Quoted in Kellerman, *Leadership*, p. 71.

23. Quoted in Kellerman, *Leadership*, p. 238.

24. Quoted in Kellerman, *Followership*, p. 44.

25. Quoted in Kellerman, *Leadership*, pp. 257, 258.

26. Paulo Freire, *Pedagogy of the Oppressed* (1970; reprint, New York: Continuum, 2005), p. 45.

27. Both cites are in Barbara Kellerman, *Reinventing Leadership: Making the Connection Between Politics and Business* (Albany: State University of New York Press, 1999), pp. 32–33.

28. David Ewing, "Who Wants Corporate Democracy?" quoted in Kellerman, *Reinventing Leadership*, p. 50.

Chapter 2: Cultural Constraints—*leveling the playing field*

1. *Amy Vanderbilt's Complete Book of Etiquette: A Guide to Gracious Living* (Garden City, NY: Doubleday, 1952). All quotes in this and the preceding paragraph are from the book.

2. C. Wright Mills, *The Power Elite* (New York: Oxford University Press, 2000).

3. Bernard M. Bass with Ruth Bass, *The Bass Handbook of Leadership: Theory, Research, and Managerial Applications* (New York: Free Press, 2008), p. 101.

4. Bass and Bass, *The Bass Handbook of Leadership*, p. 460.

5. Joseph C. Rost, *Leadership for the Twenty-First Century* (New York: Praeger, 1991), p. 94.

6. Philip Selznick, *Leadership in Administration: A Sociological Interpretation* (Berkeley: University of California Press, 1957), p. 24.

7. David Brooks, "The Quest for Dignity," *New York Times*, February 1, 2011, p. A27.

8. Barbara Kellerman, *Followership: How Followers Are Creating Change and Changing Leaders* (Boston: Harvard Business School Press, 2008).

9. Judith Martin, *Miss Manners' Guide to Excruciatingly Correct Behavior* (New York: Norton, 2005), p. 469. Other quotes and similar ones, passim.

10. Warren Bennis, *On Becoming a Leader* (New York: Perseus, 2003), pp. 39, 40.

11. James M. Kouzes and Barry Z. Posner, *The Leadership Challenge* (San Francisco: Jossey-Bass, 2007), pp. 223–34.

12. Bill George, *Authentic Leadership: Rediscovering the Secrets to Lasting Value* (San Francisco: Jossey-Bass, 2003), p. 91.

13. Daniel Goleman, *Primal Leadership: Realizing the Power of Emotional Intelligence* (Cambridge, MA: Harvard Business School Press, 2002), pp. 173, 189.

14. Goleman, *Primal Leadership*, p. 69.

15. Diane Brady, "Charm Offensive: Why America's CEOs Are Suddenly So Eager to Be Loved," *BusinessWeek*, June 26, 2006, p. 26.

16. Ori Brafman and Rod A. Beckstrom, *The Starfish and the Spider: The Unstoppable Power of Leaderless Organizations* (New York: Portfolio, 2006), p. 7.

17. John F. Harris, *The Survivor: Bill Clinton in the White House* (New York: Random House, 2005), p. 293.

18. Coverage of the trials of Mayor Michael Bloomberg was extensive during this period. See, for example, *New York Times*, December 31, 2010.

19. Jennifer Senior wrote an excellent account of the saga of Bob Kerrey at the New School in "Bob Kerrey's Ivory-Tower War," *New York*, February 22, 2009.

20. Vineet Nayar, *Employees First, Customers Second* (Boston: Harvard Business Press, 2010). Quotes are on pp. 13, 65, and 156.

Chapter 3: Technological Imperatives—*losing control*

1. T. H. Breen, *American Insurgents, American Patriots: The Revolution of the People* (New York: Hill & Wang, 2010), p. 99ff.

2. Harlan Cleveland, *Leadership and the Information Revolution*, World Academy of Art & Science, 1997, pp. 8, 24. The term "people power" was first coined in the Philippines, during the political upheavals of the 1980s.

3. Cleveland, *Leadership and the Information Revolution*, p. 26.

4. This point is made by Joseph S. Nye Jr., *The Future of Power* (New York: Public Affairs, 2011), p. 116.

5. The quote is from Raffi Khatchadourian, in Christian Caryl, "Why WikiLeaks Changes Everything," *New York Review of Books*, January 13, 2011, p. 27.

6. Nelson D. Schwartz, "Facing a New Type of Threat from WikiLeaks, a Bank Plays Defense," *New York Times*, January 3, 2011, p. B1.

7. James Herron and Will Connors, "WikiLeaks Touches Shell," *Wall Street Journal*, December 10, 2010, p. B4.

8. Richard Perez-Pena, "Web Sites That Dig for News Rise as Community Watchdogs," *New York Times*, November 18, 2008.

9. Charles Levinson, "Palestinians Blast Leaks Showing Peace-Talks Concessons," *Wall Street Journal*, January 25, 2011, p. A11.

10. James Kirchick, "WikiLeaks' Collateral Damage," *Wall Street Journal*, December 31, 2010, p. A11.

11. David Carr, "A Year of Tweeting: Why Twitter Will Endure," *New York Times*, January 3, 2010, p. 1.

12. Mark Harris wrote of the incident that Hastings "found himself scripting a blog apology so drenched in strained self-abasement" that it resulted in more than 27,000 largely acid rejoinders. In *New York*, October 24, 2011, p. 14.

13. John Schwartz, "As Jurors Turn to Web, Mistrials Are Popping Up," *New York Times*, March 18, 2009.

14. Rami G. Khouri, "When Arabs Tweet," *New York Times*, July 22, 2010.

15. "What's Next, Gen X?" Tommyerickson.com/publications.

16. Speech by Admiral Gary Roughead delivered on June 6, 2011, posted on http://thebrowser.com.

17. Erik Qualman, "3 Reasons Why CEOs Hate Social Media," *Socialnomics*, August 9, 2010.

18. Lance Whitney, "Most CEOs Not Tapping into Social Media," *CNET News*, October 13, 2010.

19. Whitney, "Most CEOs Not Tapping Into Social Media"; Quy Huy and Andrew Shipov, "Social Media's Leadership Challenges," *Harvard Business Review*, The Conversation blog, November 1, 2010.

20. Roughead speech.

21. Chris Perry, quoted in Whitney, "Most CEO's Not Tapping into Social Media."

22. David Kirkpatrick and David Sanger, "A Tunisian-Egyptian Link that Shook Arab History," *New York Times*, February 14, 2011, p. A9.

23. Guobin Yang, *The Power of the Internet in China: Citizen Activism Online* (New York: Columbia University Press, 2009), p. 13.

24. Yang, *The Power of the Internet in China*, pp. 31–33.

25. Malcolm Gladwell, "Small Change," *New Yorker*, October 4, 2010, p. 49.

26. Clay Shirky, "The Political Power of Social Media," *Foreign Affairs*, January/February 2011, p. 30. Also see Shirky, *Here Comes Everybody: The Power of Organizing Without Organizations* (New York: Penguin, 2008).

27. Evgeny Morozov, *The Net Delusion* (New York: PublicAffairs, 2011).

28. Steve Coll, "The Internet: For Better or for Worse," *New York Review of Books*, April 7, 2011, p. 20.

29. Micah L. Sifry, "Point-and-Click Politics," *Wall Street Journal*, October 30–31, 2010, p. C3.

30. Barbara Kellerman, *Followership: How Followers Are Creating Change and Changing Leaders* (Boston: Harvard Business School Press, 2008), p. 151.

31. David Barboza and Keith Bradsher, "A Labor Movement Enabled by Technology," *New York Times*, June 17, 2010, p. B1.

32. David Carr, "Online, a Nation of Serfs," *New York Times*, February 14, 2011.

33. Quotes in this paragraph are in Maureen Dowd, "Stars and Sewers," *New York Times*, February 20, 2011, p. 11.

34. John Heilemann, "Caught in Their Web," *New York*, December 20–27, 2010, p. 28.

35. Ori Brafman and Rod A. Beckstrom, *The Starfish and the Spider: The Unstoppable Power of Leaderless Organizations* (New York: Portfolio, 2006), p. 98.

36. Joseph S. Nye Jr., *The Future of Power* (New York: PublicAffairs, 2011), pp. 124, 125.

Chapter 4: Social Contract—*undermining the understanding*

1.   Mark van Vugt and Anjana Ahuja, *Naturally Selected: The Evolutionary Science of Leadership* (New York: Harper Business, 2011).

2.   For a splendid recent discussion of "charisma," see Zachary Woolfe, "A Gift from the Musical Gods, *New York Times*, August 21, 20011. Woolfe notes that while charisma in culture has been much less explored than, for example, charisma as a political phenomenon, it applies to performers of all sorts, not only to leaders. Charisma, he writes, "depends on physical presence. [It] operates most strongly on a visual level; it's telling that when we need another way of describing some-one in possession of it, we say, 'You can't take your eyes off her.' "

3.   My description here of what happened in the Boston Archdiocese in 2002 is taken from chapter 7 of my book, *Followership: How Followers Are Creating Change and Changing Leaders* (Boston: Harvard Business School Press, 2008), pp. 151–77.

4.   Russell Shorto, "The Irish Affliction," *New York Times Magazine*, February 13, 2011, pp. 44ff.

5.   Rachel Donadio, "Pope Issues His Most Direct Words to Date on Abuse," *New York Times*, May 11, 2010.

6.   Laurie Goodstein and David M. Halbfinger, "Amid Sexual Abuse Scan dal, an Office That Failed to Act," *New York Times*, July 2, 2010, p. 1.

7.   George C. Edwards III, "Strategic Assessments: Evaluating Opportunities and Strategies in the Obama Presidency," Paper delivered at the 2010 Annual Meeting of the American Political Science Association,

8.   Cornel West, "Dr. King Weeps from His Grave," *New York Times*, August 26, 2011.

9.   It's been hard for shareholder activists even to catch a break. In 2011 they were dealt a further blow by the courts, which threw out a controversial new Securities and Exchange Commission regulation intended to give investors more power to oust corporate directors.

10.   Steven M. Davidoff, "Efforts to Rein in Executive Pay Meet with Little Success," *New York Times*, July 13, 2011.

11.   Steven M. Davidoff, "Quiet Proxy Season Means Fewer Fights in the Boardroom, *New York Times*, May 4, 2011, p. B5. Davidoff cautions against concluding shareholder activism is on the upswing. For a different view, see

Jason Zweig, "Will New Tools Help Small Shareholders Topple Giants?," *Wall Street Journal*, January 7, 2012.

12.   Tilde Herrera, "Shareholder Activism Grows During Latest Proxy Season," *Greenbiz.com,* February 24, 2011.

13.   Andrew Dowell and Joann S. Lublin, "Strings Attached to Options Grant for GE's Immelt," *Wall Street Journal*, April 20, 2011. p. B1.

14.   Jennifer Liberto, "CEO Pay: Shareholders Get a (Little) Say," *CNNMoney* .com, April 21, 2011. Anyone interested in the subject of shareholder activism, might also want to follow the fortunes of a company based in Sandusky, Ohio, called Cedar Fair.

15.   Rhea Wessel, "Activist Investors Turn to Social Media to Enlist Support," *NYTimes.com*, March, 24, 2011.

16.   Wessel, "Activist Investors Turn to Social Media to Enlist Support." Other online sites that seek to rally shareholders include United States Proxy Exchange and Proxy Democracy.

17.   Miguel Bustillo, "Wal-Mart to Settle 63 Suits over Wages," *Wall Street Journal*, December 24, 2010.

18.   The Supreme Court decision in this case was widely covered, for example in the *New York Times*, June 21, 2011. Dukes's quote was on p. B4.

19.   "Make Wall Street Risk It All," *New York Times,* October 8, 2010.

20.   Josh Lowensohn, "Lawsuit Accuses Apple, Others of Fixing Worker Pay," *CNET News, Politics and Law*, May 4, 2011.

21.   Nicholas D. Kristof, "D.I.Y. Foreign-Aid Revolution," *New York Times Magazine*, October 24, 2010, pp. 49ff.

22.   Daniel Bergner, "Networker on a Mission," *New York Times Magazine*, December 5, 2010, pp. 48ff.

23.   Anand Giridharadas, "The Caste Buster," *New York Times Magazine*, January 2, 2011, pp. 37ff.

24.   Enrique Krauze, "Can This Poet Save Mexico?" *New York Times*, October 2, 2011.

Chapter 5: American Experience—*downgrading leaders*

1.   Alan Pell Crawford, "A Revolution from Below," *Wall Street Journal*, May 21, 2010, p. W4.

2. Jane Mansbridge, "A 'Selection Model' of Political Representation," *Journal of Political Philosophy* 17, no. 4 (2009), p. 371.

3. Michael Tomasky, "The Specter Haunting the Senate," *New York Review of Books*, September 30, 2010, p. 22.

4. George Packer, "The Empty Chamber," *New Yorker*, August 9, 2010, p. 45.

5. Norman Ornstein, "A Filibuster Fix," *New York Times*, August 28, 2010.

6. Study by Alan Abramovitz, quoted in David Gergen and Michael Zuckerman, "Is America Becoming a House Divided Against Itself?" on *CNN Opinion*, September 28, 2011.

7. Andrew Hacker, "The Next Election: The Surprising Reality," *New York Review of Books*, August 18, 2011, p. 78.

8. Daniel Stone, "Hail to the Chiefs," *Newsweek*, November 27, 2010, p. 29.

9. Frank Rich, "Why Has He Fallen Short?," *New York Review of Books*, August 19, 2010, p. 8.

10. Rich, "Why Has He Fallen Short?" p. 8.

11. Peter Baker, "What Does He Do Now?" *New York Times Magazine*, October 17, 2010, p. 45.

12. Sudhir Venkatesh, "Feeling Too Down to Rise Up," *New York Times*, March 29, 2009.

13. John Heilemann and Mark Halperin, *Game Change: Obama and the Clintons, McCain and Palin, and the Race of a Lifetime* (New York: HarperCollins, 2010), p. 33.

14. Heilemann and Halperin, *Game Change*, pp. 37, 5, 6.

15. Again, the reference here is to the types of followers as described in my book *Followership: How Followers Are Creating Change and Changing Leaders* (Boston: Harvard Business School Press, 2008).

16. Joe Trippi quoted in Claire Cain Miller, "How Obama's Internet Campaign Changed Politics," *New York Times*, November 7, 2008.

17. See Gordon Wood, "No Thanks for the Memories," *New York Review of Books*, January 13, 2011, p. 40. Wood reviews a book on the Tea Party by Jill Lepore, *The Whites of Their Eyes: The Tea Party's Revolution and the Battle of American History*.

18. Kate Zernike, *Boiling Mad: Inside Tea Party America* (New York: Times Books, 2010), p. 6. This is a good account of the rise of the Tea Party and particularly of how ordinary people stitched it together out of whole cloth. Also see Theda Skocpol and Vanessa Williamson, *The Tea Party and the Remaking of Conservatism* (New York: Oxford University Press, 2012).

19. Douglas A. Blackman et al., "Birth of a Movement," *Wall Street Journal*, October 29, 2010, p. 1.

20. Matt Bai, "D.I.Y. Populism, Left and Right," *New York Times*, October 31, 2010.

21. David E. Campbell and Robert D. Putnam, "Crashing the Tea Party," *New York Times*, August 18, 2011.

22. Peter J. Boyer, "House Rule," *New Yorker*, December 13, 2010.

23. Jason Ahmadi, a spokesman for Occupy Wall Street, quoted in Andrew Grossman and Jessica Firger, " 'Leaderless' Group Organizes" in *Wall Street Journal*, October 10, 2011. Also see Mattathias Schwartz, "Pre-Occupied," *New Yorker*, November 28, 2011.

24. Gallup Poll, February 1, 2011.

25. Cited by Gerald Seib, "Populist Anger over Economy Carries Risks for Big Business," in *Wall Street Journal*, October 11, 2011.

26. James Surowiecki, "Soak the Very, Very Rich," *New Yorker*, August 14 and 23, 2010, p. 33.

27. Jay Lorsch and Rakesh Khurana, "The Pay Problem," *Harvard Magazine*, May–June 2010.

28. *Forbes*, Special Report, CEO Compensation, April 30, 2008.

29. Jessica Silver-Greenberg and Alexis Leondis, "How Much Is a CEO Worth?" *Blooomberg Businessweek*, May 10–16, 2010.

30. David Carr, "Why Not Occupy Newsrooms?" *New York Times*, October 24, 2011, p. B1.

31. Jospeh E. Stiglitz, "Of the 1%, by the 1%, for the 1%," *Vanity Fair*, May 2011, p. 126.

32. Jim Rutenberg and Megan Thee-Brenan, "New Poll Shows Darkening Mood Across America," *New York Times*, April 22, 2011, p. A1. The disappearing American Dream also implies a broken social contract (see chapter 4). For more on the economic infringement on this arrangement, see George Packer, "The Broken Contract," *Foreign Affairs*, November/December 2011.

33. Floyd Norris, "Crisis Is Over; but Where's the Fix?" *New York Times*, March 11, 2011, p. B1.

34. James Jurowiecki, "Board Stiff," *New Yorker*, June 1, 2009, p. 34.

35. Quoted in Michael Skapinker, "Narcissistic Leaders Need External Controls," *Financial Times*, April 29, 2009.

36. John Kay, "Beware the Cult of the Heroic Chief Executive," *Financial Times*, June 9, 2010.

37. Jason Zweig, "Why Turning the Page on a CEO Isn't Always a Panacea," *Wall Street Journal*, December 10, 2009, p. A11.

38. Diane Brady, "Can GE Still Manage?," *Bloomberg Businessweek*, April 26, 2010, p. 27.

39. Graydon Carter, "Dimon in the Rough," *Vanity Fair*, April 2011, p. 66.

40. Deborah L. Rhode, "Introduction: Where Is the Leadership in Moral Leadership?," in Deborah L. Rhode, ed., *Moral Leadership: The Theory and Practice of Power, Judgment, and Policy* (San Francisco: Jossey-Bass, 2007), p. 37.

41. See James B. Stewart for an articulate expression of outrage over the lack of punishment for Tyson officials, "Bribery, but Nobody Was Charged," *New York Times*, June 25, 2011.

42. "The Worst Managers," *BusinessWeek*, January 19, 2009.

43. Julie Creswell and Louise Story, "Thain Resigns Amid Losses at Bank of America," *New York Times*, January 23, 2009.

44. Gretchen Morgenson, "How Countrywide Covered the Tracks," *New York Times*, October 17, 2010, p. BU8.

45. The words are those of Michigan senator Carl Levin in Floyd Norris, "Eyes Open, WaMu Still Failed," *New York Times*, March 25, 2011, p. B1.

46. Ezra Klein, "Washington's Suicide Pact," *Newsweek*, March 21, 2011, p. 7.

47. Evan Thomas, "We the Problem," *Newsweek*, February 25, 2010.

48. Christopher Hayes, "The Twilight of the Elites," *Time*, May 23, 2010, p. 56.

49. Kurt Andersen, "Is Democracy Killing Democracy?" *New York*, February 5, 2010, p. 20.

Chapter 6: Worldwide Momentum—*upgrading followers*

1. Peter Grier, "Global Spread of Democracy Stalled," *Christian Science Monitor*, November 21, 2007.

2. Ronald Inglehart and Christian Welzel, "How Development Leads to Democracy," *Foreign Affairs*, April 2009, p. 33.

3. Inglehart and Welzel, "How Development Leads to Democracy," p. 34.

4. Frank Dikotter, *Mao's Great Famine: The History of China's Most Devastating Catastrophe, 1958–1962* (New York: Walker, 2010).

5. Stéphane Courtois et al., *The Black Book of Communism: Crimes, Terror, Repression* (Cambridge, MA: Harvard University Press, 1999). The title of this section of my chapter is drawn from the title of this book.

6. Zbigniew Brzezinski, *Out of Control: Global Turmoil on the Eve of the 21st Century* (New York: Scribner's, 1993).

7. Zbigniew Brzezinski, *The Grand Failure: The Birth and Death of Communism in the Twentieth Century* (New York: Scribner's, 1989), p. 220.

8. Andrew Osborn and Alan Cullison, "Oil's Crash Stirs Unrest in Russia as Slump Hits Home," *Wall Street Journal*, December 19, 2010, p. 1. Also see David Remnick, "The Civil Archipelago," *New Yorker*, December 19 and 26, 2011.

9. Julia Ioffe, "Net Impact," *New Yorker*, April 4, 2011, p. 27.

10. Aleh Tsyvinski, quoted in Ioffe, "Net Impact," p. 31. Also see Andrew E. Kramer, "Russian Site Smokes Out Corruption, *New York Times*, March 27, 2011.

11. The quotes in this paragraph and the next are all from Ian Johnson, "The Party: Impenetrable, All Powerful," *New York Review of Books*, September 30, 2010, p. 69.

12. Quoted in Tom Mitchell, "Factory Workers Swap Angst for Anger," *Financial Times*, June 1, 2010, p. 3.

13. James Glanz and John Markoff, "Vast Hacking by a China Fearful of Web," *New York Times*, December 5, 2010, p. 1.

14. Sharon LaFraniere and David Barboza, "China Tightens Censorship of Electronic Communications," *New York Times*, March 22, 2011.

15. Andrew Jacobs and Jonathan Ansfield, "Well-Oiled Security Apparatus in China Stifles Calls for Change," *New York Times*, March 1, 2011, p. A1.

16. Scott Sayare, "As Web Challenges French Leaders, They Push Back," *New York Times*, December 13, 2009.

17. Stephen Erlanger, "Amid Protests and Strikes French Leader Vows Order," *New York Times*, October 20, 2010, p. A10.

18. Suzanne Daley, "A Political Awakening That Keeps Them Up All Night," *New York Times*, June 7, 2011, p. A4.

19. Reuters, September 2, 2011.

20. Marcus Walker et al., "Euro-Zone Leaders Feel Fallout from Crises," *Wall Street Journal*, July 6, 2010, p. A6. The complaints against Merkel grew, along with the debt crisis in Europe. One commentator wrote, "Merkel is failing to secure German demands in Europe, and she has not succeeded in winning Germans over to the rescue of the Euro." Alan Cowell, "Scrutiny of German Leader Builds as Debt Crisis Rattles Europe," *New York Times*, June 20, 2011, p. A6.

21. Nicholas Kulish, "Pirates' Strong Showing in Regional Elections Surprises Even Them," *New York Times*, September 20, 2011, p. A5.

22. "A Decade of Convergence and Compression," *European CEO*, July 16, 2010.

23. Martin Fackler, "Parade of Prime Ministers Has Japan Still Searching for a Route out of Recession," *New York Times*, June 15, 2010, p. A8.

24. Joshua Hammer, "A Free Woman," *New Yorker*, January 24, 2011, pp. 24ff.

25. Norimitsu Onishi, "Internet Grows in Indonesia, as Does a Debate on Its Limits," *New York Times*, April 20, 2010.

26. Ashutosh Varshney, quoted by Lydia Polgreen, "New Business Class Rises in Ashes of South India's Caste System," *New York Times*, September 11, 2010.

27. Amol Sharma, "In India, the Supreme Court Takes a More Activist Role," *Wall Street Journal*, May 16, 2011.

28. The phrase "seemingly overnight" was taken from a headline in the *Harvard University Gazette*, March 28–April 6, 2011, p. 12.

29. Simon Sebag Montefiore, "Every Revolution Is Revolutionary in Its Own Way," *New York Times*, March 27, 2011, p. WK11.

30. Samantha M. Shapiro, "Can Social Networking Turn Disaffected Young Egyptians into a Force for Democratic Change?," *New York Times Magazine*, January 25, 2009, pp. 32ff.

31. Steve Coll, "The Casbah Revolution," *New Yorker*, April 4, 2011, pp. 34ff.

32. "Volcano of Rage," *New York Review of Books*, March 24, 2011, pp. 4ff.

33. For a more detailed account of the early events in Syria, see Nour Malas, "Syria Revolt Fueled by Roof Fires and Tweets," *Wall Street Journal*, July 15, 2011, p. A1.

34. Steve Coll, "The Syrian Problem," *New Yorker*, May 30, 2011, p. 23.

35. Marc Lynch, quoted by Robert E. Worth and David D. Kirkpatrick, "Seizing a Moment, Al Jazeera Galvanizes Arab Frustration," *New York Times*, January 28, 2011, p. A1.

36. The phrase in quotes is from Montefiore. Also see Kareem Fahim and Mona El-Naggar, "Some Fear a Street Movement's Leaderless Status May Become a Liability," *New York Times*, February 4, 2011.

37. "1989!," *New York Review of Books*, November 5, 2009, pp. 4ff.

Chapter 7: Leadership Industry—*leading as mantra*

1. In an article published in 2007, Doris Gomez writes, "Annual corporate spending on leadership development has risen to $45 billion from $10 billion in the mid-1980s. Reports from the training industry say that nearly $50 billion is spent annually on corporate training and development." However, Gomez takes her figures from earlier work, published in 1997. This means the figures now, in the second decade of the twenty-first century, are much higher. See Gomez, "The Leader as Learner," *International Journal of Leadership Studies* 2, no. 3 (2007).

2. Scott Snook, Nitin Nohria, Rakesh Khurana, *The Handbook for Teaching Leadership: Knowing, Doing, Being* (New York: Russell Sage, 2011), p. xi.

3. Quoted in Barbara Kellerman, *Bad Leadership: What It Is, How It Happens, Why It Matters* (Boston: Harvard Business School Press, 2004), p. 3.

4. Barbara Kellerman and Deborah Rhode, eds., *Women and Leadership: State of Play and Strategies for Change* (San Francisco: Jossey-Bass, 2007) and Nitin Nohria and Rakesh Khurana, eds., *Handbook of Leadership Theory and Practice* (Boston: Harvard Business Press, 2010). Additionally, in 2011, Sage published *The Handbook for Teaching Leadership*, edited by Nitin Nohria, Rakesh Khurana, and Scott Snook.

5. Nohria and Khurana, eds., *Handbook of Leadership Theory*, p. 4.

6. For more on leadership in the U.S. Army, see *Be, Know, Do—Leadership the Army Way*, adapted from the official Army Leadership Manual (San Francisco: Jossey-Bass, 2004).

7. For a full discussion of these various programs see Meredith L. Gore and Shawn J. Riley, "Are Leadership Programs Cultivating Tomorrow's Leaders in Wildlife Management?" in *Human Dimensions of Wildlife* 14 (2009), pp. 149–51.

8. Ann Scheck McAlearney, "Executive Leadership Development in U.S.

Healthcare Systems: Exploring the Evidence," report prepared for the American College of Healthcare Executives, 2008.

9. Maureen C. Trott and Kim Windsor, "Leadership Effectiveness: How Do You Measure UP?" *Nursing Economics*, May–June 1999, p. 127.

10. Rakesh Khurana, *From Higher Aims to Hired Hands: The Social Transformation of American Business Schools and the Unfulfilled Promise of Management as a Profession* (Princeton, NJ: Princeton University Press, 2007), p. 4.

11. Khurana, *From Higher Aims to Hired Hands*, p. 5.

12. The information in this paragraph is from Kim Lamoureux et al., "Leadership Development Factbook—2009," Bersin & Associates, October 2009.

13. "Best Companies for Leadership," *Bloomberg Businessweek*, February 16, 2010.

14. The quotes are from GE's leadership development website.

15. *2009–2010 Annual Report*, Center for Creative Leadership, p. 25.

16. Ellen Van Velsor et al., *The Center for Creative Leadership Handbook of Leadership Development* (San Francisco: Jossey Bass, 2010), p. xviii.

17. Among the most careful researchers in this general regard is Bruce Avolio. See, for example, Bruce J. Avolio et al., "A Meta-analytic Review of Leadership Impact Research: Experimental and Quasi-experimental Studies," *Leadership Quarterly* 20 (2009), pp. 764–84. Also see Bruce J. Avolio et al., "Estimating Return on Leadership Development Investment," *Leadership Quarterly* 21 (2010), pp. 633–44.

18. *National Leadership Index*, Center for Public Leadership, Harvard University, 2011.

19. Second Annual State of the American Dream Survey, Xavier University, March 2011.

20. Maritz Poll, Maritz Research, April 17, 2010.

21. Frank Bruni, "The Fall This Summer," *New York Times*, August 28, 2011.

22. Shawn Tully, "Is Goldman a Dinosaur?" *CNNMoney*, November 2, 2010, http://finance.fortune.cnn.com/2010/11/02/is-goldman-a-dinosaur/.

23. The quote is from Jessica Pressler, "It's Too Bad. And I Don't Mean It's Too Bad Like 'Screw 'Em,' " *New York*, August 1, 2011, p. 25.

24. Survey by Korn/Ferry in *Economic Times*, April 15, 2010.

25. Alan Murray, "Supervising Success," *Wall Street Journal*, December 8, 2010, p. A21.

26. Kate Linebaugh, "Immelt and GE, 10 Years In," *Wall Street Journal*, September 6, 2011.

27. For more on bad leadership, see Barbara Kellerman, *Bad Leadership: What It Is, How It Happens, Why It Matters* (Boston: Harvard Business School Press, 2004).

28. "The Worst Managers," *BusinessWeek*, January 19, 2009.

29. Joe Nocera, "Inquiry Is Missing Bottom Line," *New York Times*, January 29, 2011, p. B7. Nocera was discussing the report on the financial crisis issued by the Financial Crisis Inquiry Commission. The report is titled *The Financial Crisis Inquiry Report*, and it is full of the sort of damning evidence that inevitably raises questions about our capacity to raise leaders.

30. Warren Bennis and James O'Toole, "How Business Schools Lost Their Way," *Harvard Business Review*, May 2005.

31. Khurana, *From Higher Aims to Hired Hands*, p. 357.

32. Jeffrey Pfeffer, *Power: Why Some People Have It—and Others Don't* (New York: HarperCollins, 2010), p. 11.

33. For more on Blair Sheppard's ideas on how to "reshape" business education, see "Reshaping Business Education in the New Era," *McKinsey Quarterly*, January 2010. Also see Robin J. Ely, Herminia Ibarra, Deborah Kolb, "Taking Gender into Account: Theory and Design for Women's Leadership Development Programs," *Academy of Management Learning and Education*, September 2011. They argue that there is no coherent framework for leadership programs for women.

34. See chapter by Richard J. Hackman, "What Is This Thing Called Leadership?," in Nohria and Khurana, eds., *Handbook of Leadership*, pp. 107–16. Also see the chapter by Joel M. Podolny et al., "Revisiting the Meaning of Leadership," pp. 65–105.

35. In the proposal for *The Handbook for Teaching Leadership*, the current state of leadership education is said to have "flaws" such as "course content [that] rarely conforms to the norms of the scientific method," teachers who "employ casual and often self-serving empirical evidence," approaches that are "rarely grounded in any well-established theoretical tradition," and "scant empirical evidence that any of these approaches really work."

Chapter 8: Leadership Complete—*leading in time*

1. Confucius, *Analects*, Chapter 2.
2. Deborah L. Rhode and Amanda K. Packel, *Leadership: Law, Policy, and Management* (New York: Wolters Kluwer, 2011), p. 219. The quote is from Max H. Bazerman and Ann E. Tenbrunsel, *Blind Spots: Why We Fail to Do What's Right and What to Do About It* (Princeton, NJ: Princeton University Press, 2011). See Bazerman and Tenbrunsel for further discussion on how to avoid ethical "blind spots." For a discussion of how some educators are trying to develop character in young people, see Paul Tough, "The Character Test" in *New York Times Magazine*, September 18, 2011, pp. 38ff.
3. Leadership scholars have acknowledged the importance of context for decades; "contingency" theories address this issue in particular. However, "contingency" nearly always refers to the proximal context, as opposed to the more distal one. Moreover, even this limited form of contextual awareness generally does not find its way into teaching "how to lead"—unless such teaching is within a particular organization or institution, in which case it, as opposed to any other context, is the focus.
4. The phrase is Richard Hackman's. See *Leading Teams: Setting the Stage for Great Performances* (Boston: Harvard Business School Press, 2002), pp. 199, 200. For a superb essay on the leader as a psychosocial construction, see Sonja M. Hunt, "The Role of Leadership in the Construction of Reality" in Barbara Kellerman, ed., *Leadership: Multidisciplinary Perspectives* (Englewood Cliffs, NJ: Prentice-Hall, 1984), pp. 157–78.
5. I have borrowed here from Rakesh Khurana, one of whose books is titled *Searching for a Corporate Savior: The Irrational Quest for Charismatic CEOs* (Princeton, NJ: Princeton University Press, 2002).
6. See, for example, John P. Kotter, *A Force for Change: How Leadership Differs from Management* (New York: Free Press, 1990).
7. John Kotter, *Leadership Without Easy Answers* (Cambridge, MA: Harvard University Press, 1994). The quote on mobilizing is from Ronald Heifetz et al., *The Practice of Adaptive Leadership* (Boston: Harvard Business Press, 2009), p. 14.
8. Bill George, *Authentic Leadership* (San Francisco: Jossey-Bass, 2003), p. 12. Robert Greenleaf's ideas have been written about widely.
9. James MacGregor Burns, *Leadership* (New York: Harper & Row, 1978), p. 20.

10. Scott Snook, Nitin Nohria, and Rakesh Khurana, eds., *The Handbook for Teaching Leadership: Knowing, Doing, and Being* (New York: Sage, 2011), p. xi.

11. For more on this, see Clayton M. Christensen and Michael B. Horn, "Colleges in Crisis," *Harvard Magazine*, July–August 2011, p. 43.

12. Boris Groysberg and Scott Snook, "Leadership Development at Goldman Sachs," Harvard Business School Case Study #9-406-002, revised March 12, 2007.

13. Shoma Chaterjee, Cary Friedman, and Keith Yardly, "Leadership Acceleration at Goldman Sachs," in Snook, Nohria, and Khurana, eds., *The Handbook for Teaching Leadership.*

14. Patricia O'Connell, "Goldman Sachs: Committed to the Next Generation," *Bloomberg Businessweek*, February 16, 2010.

15. Carol Pledger, "Building Manager Effectiveness by Combining Leadership Training and Organization Development," *Organizational Development Journal* (Spring 2007), pp. 71ff.

16. Adam Bryant, "Lessons Learned at Goldman," *New York Times*, September 13, 2009.

17. Unless otherwise sourced, the material on GE is available on the Web.

18. Glenn Rowe, Roderick White, Derek Lehmberg, and John Phillips, "General Electric: An Outlier in CEO Talent Development," *Ivey Business Journal*, January/February 2009.

19. Brett Arends, "GE Has Been an Investor Disaster under Jeff Immelt," *Marketwatch*, March 8, 2010; Peter Cohan, "GE's Business Model Is Broken, and Jeff Immelt Hasn't Fixed It," *Daily Finance*, April 16, 2010. See also Kate Linebaugh, "Tea-Party Attacks Put GE on the Defense," *Wall Street Journal*, October 10, 2011.

20. Jeffrey Immelt, "Renewing American Leadership," speech delivered at U.S. Military Academy, West Point, NY, December 9, 2009.

21. Carolyn April, "IBM's Commitment to Employee Leadership a Lesson for All," *Channel Insider Blog*, November 30, 2009.

22. Tim Ringo, Allan Schweyer, Michael DeMarco, Ross Jones, and Eric Lesser, "Integrated Talent Management," IBM Corporation, 2008.

23. "The Enterprise of the Future: Implications for the Workforce," Global CEO Study, IBM Corporation, 2008.

24. IBM CIO Leadership Exchange, Shanghai, February 2009, and IBM CIO

Leadership Exchange, "Bringing Together the World's Leading CIO's," Barcelona, March 2010.

25. Tom Kucharvy, blog posting dated January 23, 2011.

26. Quote is from Kucharvy. The evaluation was done by a professor at the Harvard Business School, Christopher Marquis. His evaluation is available on the Web.

27. Thom Shanker, "Win Wars? Today's General Must Also Meet, Manage, Placate, Politick and Do P.R.," *New York Times*, August 13, 2010, p. A11.

28. Barbara Kellerman, *Bad Leadership: What It Is, How It Happens, Why It Matters* (Boston: Harvard Business School Press, 2004), pp. 169ff.

29. Jesse Eisinger, "In Goldman Sachs's Short on Housing, a Misdirection," *New York Times*, June 16, 2011, p. B6.

30. Todd L. Pittinsky, ed., *Crossing the Divide: Intergroup Leadership in a World of Difference* (Boston: Harvard Business Press, 2009).

31. Bazerman and Tenbrunsel, *Blind Spots*, p. 7.

32. Morton T. Hansen, Herminia Ibarra, and Urs Peyer, "The Best-Performing CEOs in the World," *Harvard Business Review*, January–February 2010, pp. 104ff.

33. Roger Thompson, "New Dean Sets Five Priorities for HBS," *Working Knowledge*, December 20, 2010.

34. Description available on website of the Accenture Leadership Center at the University of Wisconsin School of Business.

35. These figures are from William Walker, "A Capitalist Idea," *New York Times*, September 7, 2011.

36. Linda Hill and Kent Lineback, *Being the Boss: The 3 Imperatives for Becoming a Great Leader* (Boston: Harvard Business Review Press, 2011).

37. Jeffrey Gandz, Marry Crossan, Gerart Seijts, and Carol Stephenson, "Leadership on Trial: A Manifesto for Leadership Development," Richard Ivey School of Business, University of Western Ontario, 2010.

38. Jim Kouzes and James Posner, *The Leadership Challenge* (San Francisco: Jossey-Bass, 2008).

39. An exception to this general rule is Grady McGonagill and Tina Doerffer, *Leadership and Web 2.0: The Leadership Implications of the Evolving Web* (Washington, DC: Bertelsmann Stiftung, 2011). This smart, slight volume is, as its title implies, dedicated to the all-important question of how the Web is impacting on leadership in the second decade of the twenty-first century.

40. From Dan Tapscott and David Ticoll, *The Naked Corporation*, quoted in Anthony Goodman, "Leadership in the Age of Wikileaks," *FT.com*, January 3, 2011. Other recent examples of corporate leaders having to backtrack include Coke (consumers forced it to switch back from white cans to red cans in a week) and the Gap (customers used online backlash to compel it to ditch its new logo).

41. Michael Skapinker, "Real Bosses Know When to Take a Beating," *FT.com*, March 21, 2011.

42. Tamara J. Erickson, "The Leaders We Need Now," *Harvard Business Review*, May 2010, p. 66.

43. Morley Winograd and Michael D. Hais, *Millennial Makeover: MySpace, YouTube & the Future of American Politics* (New Brunswick, NJ: Rutgers University Press, 2008).

44. "Managing the Facebookers," *Economist*, January 3, 2009, p. 10.

45. Soumitra Dutta, "What's Your Personal Media Strategy?" *Harvard Business Review*, November 2010, p. 127.

46. Josh Bernoff and Ted Schadler, "Empowered," *Harvard Business Review*, July–August 2010, p. 95.

47. Venkat Ramaswamy and Francis Gouillart, "Building the Co-Creative Enterprise," *Harvard Business Review*, October 2010, pp. 100ff.

48. "Restoring Confidence in Business: Not Just about Shareholders," *Wall Street Journal*, November 22, 2010, p. R3.

49. Sharon Begley, "Weather Panic: This Is the New Normal," *Newsweek*, June 6, 2011.

50. John Cassidy, "Prophet Motive," *New Yorker*, February 28, 2011, p. 34.

51. David Brooks, "Pundit Under Protest," *New York Times*, June 14, 2010.

52. The figures are from Begley, "Weather Panic," and Brooks, "Pundit Under Protest."

53. See, for example, Joe Nocera's op-ed titled "What Is Business Waiting For?" *New York Times*, August 16, 2011, in which Nocera argues that since government is "essentially paralyzed for the foreseeable future," business should pick up the slack, particularly as it applies to the problem of high unemployment. I like the idea, but from where, exactly, is this sort of bold corporate leadership supposed to emanate? So far anyway, there has been no evidence that business leaders, any more than political leaders, have the will and/or skill to lead such a charge.

54. David Greenberg, "No Exit," *New York Times Book Review*, March 20, 2011, p. 31.

Index

About the Author

Barbara Kellerman is the James MacGregor Burns Lecturer in Public Leadership at Harvard University's John F. Kennedy School of Government. She was the founding executive director of the Kennedy School's Center for Public Leadership and served as its research director. She was ranked by Forbes.com among the Top 50 Business Thinkers in 2009, and by *Leadership Excellence* in the top 15 of 100 "best minds on leadership" in 2008 and 2009. In 2010 she was given the Wilbur M. McFeeley Award for her pioneering work on leadership and followership. She is author and editor of many books, including, most recently, *Bad Leadership*, *Followership*, and *Leadership: Essential Selections on Power, Authority, and Influence*.